"Whatever your occupation may be, and however crowded your hours with affairs, do not fail to secure at least a few minutes every day for refreshment of your inner life with a bit of poetry."

POEMS

YOU OUGHT TO KNOW

SELECTED BY

ELIA WILKINSON PEATTIE

———

ILLUSTRATED BY
ELLSWORTH YOUNG

———

Granger Index Reprint Series

BOOKS FOR LIBRARIES PRESS
FREEPORT, NEW YORK

First Published 1902
Reprinted 1969

STANDARD BOOK NUMBER:
8369-6085-8

LIBRARY OF CONGRESS CATALOG CARD NUMBER:
75-98084

INTRODUCTION.

Each morning, for several months, the CHICAGO TRIBUNE nas published at the head of its first column, a poem under the caption: "Poems You Ought to Know." It has explained its action by the following quotation from a remark by Professor Charles Eliot Norton:

"Whatever your occupation may be, and however crowded your hours with affairs, do not fail to secure at least a few minutes every day for refreshment of your inner life with a bit of poetry."

By publishing these poems THE TRIBUNE hoped to accomplish two things: first; to inspire a love of poetry in the hearts of many of its readers who have never before taken time or thought to read the best poems of this and other centuries and lands; to remind those who have once loved song, but forgotten it among the sturdier voices of the world, of the melody that enchanted them in their youth.

The title has carried with it its own standard, and the poems have been kept on a plane above jocularity or mere prettiness of versification; rather have they tried to teach the doctrines of courage, of nature-love, of pure and noble melody It has been the ambition of those who selected the verses to choose something which would lift the reader above the "petty round of irritating concerns and duties," and the object will have been achieved if it has helped anyone to "play the man," "to go blithely about his business all the day," with a consciousness of the abounding beauty which dwells in the world of thought, and which is the common property of all men.

No anthology of English verse can be complete, and none can satisfy all. The compiler's individual taste, tempered and guided by established authority, is almost the only standard. This collection has been compiled not by one but by many thousands, and their selections here appear edited and winnowed as the idea of the series seemed to dictate. The book appears at the wide-spread and almost universal request of those who have watched the bold and unique experiment of a great Twentieth Century American newspaper giving the place of honor in its columns every day to a selection from the poets.

For permission to reprint certain poems by Longfellow, Lowell, Harte, Hay, Bayard Taylor, Holmes, Whittier, Parsons, and Aldrich, graciously accorded by Houghton, Mifflin & Co., the publishers, thanks are gratefully acknowledged. To Charles Scribner's Sons, for an extract from Lañier's poems, and lastly to the many thousand readers, who, by their sympathy, appreciation and help have encouraged the continuance of the daily publication of the poems, similar gratitude is felt.

CONTENTS

CONTENTS.

CONTENTS.

TO SLEEP.

BY WILLIAM WORDSWORTH.

William Wordsworth was born in 1770 and died at Rydal Mount in 1850. He was educated in Cambridge, where he graduated in 1791. He traveled on the continent before that, but he settled down for several years in Dorset. A visit from Coleridge determined his career in 1796. He was again abroad in 1798, but returned the following year and went to live at Grasmere in the lake district. He held several government positions and was poet laureate from 1843 to his death. His chief works are, "The Evening Walk," "Descriptive Sketches," "The Excursion," "White Doe of Rylston," "Thanksgiving Ode," "Peter Bell," "Waggoner," "River Duddon," A Series of Sonnets, "The Borderers," "Yarrow Revisited," and "The Prelude."

A flock of sheep that leisurely pass by
   One after one; the sound of rain, and bees
   Murmuring; the fall of rivers, winds and seas,
Smooth fields, white sheets of water, and pure sky;

I've thought of all by turns, and still I lie
   Sleepless; and soon the small birds' melodies
   Must hear, first utter'd from my orchard trees,
And the first cuckoo's melancholy cry.

Even thus last night and two nights more I lay,
   And could not win thee, Sleep, by any stealth;
So do not let me wear tonight away;
   Without thee what is all the morning's wealth?
Come, blessed barrier between day and day,
   Dear mother of fresh thoughts and joyous health!

THE OLD FAMILIAR FACES.

BY CHARLES LAMB.

Charles Lamb was born at London in 1775. His most successful writings are the "Tales from Shakespeare" (written in collaboration with his sister), and his "Essays of Elia." Lamb died in 1834.

I have had playmates, I have had companions,
In my days of childhood, in my joyful school days—
All, all are gone, the old familiar faces.

I have been laughing, I have been carousing,
Drinking late, sitting late, with my bosom cronies—
All, all are gone, the old familiar faces.

I loved a love once, fairest among women;
Closed are her doors on me, I must not see her—
All, all are gone the old familiar faces.

I have a friend, a kinder friend has no man;
Like an ingrate, I left my friend abruptly;
Left him to muse on the old familiar faces.

Ghost-like I pace round the haunts of my childhood,
Earth seemed a desert I was bound to traverse,
Seeking to find the old familiar faces.

Friend of my bosom, thou more than a brother,
Why wert not thou born in my father's dwelling?
So might we talk of the old familiar faces—

How some they have died, and some they have left me,
And some are taken from me; all are departed—
All, all are gone, the old familiar faces.

WHEN IN DISGRACE.

BY WILLIAM SHAKSPEARE.

When in disgrace with fortune and men's eyes,
   I all alone beweep my outcast state,
And trouble deaf heaven with my bootless cries,
   And look upon myself and curse my fate,
Wishing me like to one more rich in hope,
   Featur'd like him, like him with friends possess'd,
Desiring this man's art and that man's scope,
   With what I most enjoy contented least;
Yet in these thoughts myself almost despising,
   Haply I think on thee and then my state,
(Like to the lark at break of day arising,
   From sullen earth), sings hymns at heaven's gate;
For thy sweet love remember'd such wealth brings
   That then I scorn to change my state with kings.

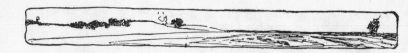

"THOUGH LOST TO SIGHT, TO MEMORY DEAR."

THOMAS MOORE.

Sweetheart, good-by! The fluttering sail
  Is spread to waft me far from thee;
And soon before the favoring gale
  My ship shall bound across the sea.
Perchance, all desolate and forlorn,
  These eyes shall miss thee many a year;
But unforgotten every charm—
  Though lost to sight, to memory dear.

Sweetheart, good-by! One last embrace!
  Oh, cruel fate, two souls to sever!
Yet in this heart's most sacred place
  Thou, thou alone, shall dwell forever.
And still shall recollection trace
  In fancy's mirror, ever near,
Each smile, each tear, upon that face—
  Though lost to sight, to memory dear.

INTRA MUROS.

BY MARY C. GILLINGTON.

At last 'tis gone, the fever of the day—
    Thank God, there comes an end to everything;
    Under the night cloud's deepened shadowing,
The noises of the city drift away
Thro' sultry streets and alleys, and the gray
    Fogs 'round the great cathedral rise and cling.
    I long and long, but no desire will bring
Against my face the keen wind salt with spray.

O, far away, green waves, your voices call;
    Your cool lips kiss the wild and weedy shore;
        And out upon the sea-line sails are brown—
White sea birds, crying, hover—soft shades fall—
    Deep waters dimple 'round the dripping oar,
        And last rays light the little fishing town.

FATE.

BY SUSAN MARR SPALDING.

Susan Marr Spalding was born in Bath, Me., and educated in a seminary there. From early girlhood she wrote verse, her sonnets being graceful and tender. At the death of her parents she lived with her uncle, a clergyman, in New York. She married Mr. Spalding, a literary man, and made her home in Philadelphia.

Two shall be born, the whole wide world apart,
And speak in different tongues, and have no thought
Each of the other's being; and have no heed;
And these, o'er unknown seas to unknown lands
Shall cross, escaping wreck; defying death;
And, all unconsciously, shape every act to this one end
That, one day, out of darkness, they shall meet
And read life's meaning in each other's eyes.

And two shall walk some narrow way of life
So nearly side by side that, should one turn
Ever so little space to right or left,
They needs must stand acknowledged face to face.
And yet, with wistful eyes that never meet.
With groping hands that never clasp; and lips
Calling in vain to ears that never hear;
They seek each other all their weary days
And die unsatisfied—and that is fate.

A HOLY NATION.

BY RICHARD REALF.

Richard Realf was born in England in 1834 of poor parents and began writing poetry at an early age. His early work attracted the attention of Tennyson, Miss Mitford, Miss Jameson, Miss Martineau, and others, and they secured the publication of his volume, "Guesses at the Beautiful." He dabbled some in sculpture, and even studied agricultural science. In 1854 he came to New York, where he wrote stories of slum life and assisted in establishing some institutions for the relief of the poor. He joined the first free soil parties moving to Kansas and was arrested. He did newspaper work until he joined John Brown's party. He was Brown's secretary of state. He was arrested in connection with the Harper's Ferry affair, enlisted in 1862, was wounded, taught a black school in South Carolina in 1867, and for years led a hand to mouth existence, all that time writing poetry, some of it of the most exquisite beauty. Family troubles resulted in his suicide in San Francisco about 1875.

Let Liberty run onward with the years,
And circle with the seasons; let her break
The tyrant's harshness, the oppressor's spears;
Bring ripened recompenses that shall make
Supreme amends for sorrow's long arrears;
Drop holy benison on hearts that ache;
Put clearer radiance into human eyes,
And set the glad earth singing to the skies.

Clean natures coin pure statutes. Let us cleanse
The hearts that beat within us; let us mow
Clear to the roots our falseness and pretense,
Tread down our rank ambitions, overthrow
Our braggart moods of puffed self-consequence,
Plow up our hideous thistles which do grow
Faster than maize in May time, and strike dead
The base infections our low greeds have bred.

BREAK, BREAK, BREAK.

BY ALFRED TENNYSON.

Alfred Tennyson was born at Lincolnshire in 1809. In 1828 he wrote, with his brother, the "Poems by Two Brothers." He went to Trinity College, Cambridge, where he met his friend, Arthur Hallam, upon whose death he wrote "In Memoriam." When Wordsworth died in 1850, the laureateship was given to Tennyson; later he was made a Baron. He died at Aldworth, on the Isle of Wight, in 1892, and has been given a place in Westminster Abbey near the grave of Chaucer. Other of his longer poems beside the one mentioned above are: "The Princess," "Maud," "Enoch Arden," and the "Idyls of the King."

Break, break, break,
  On thy cold gray stones, O, sea!
And I would that my tongue could utter
  The thoughts that arise in me.

O, well for the fisherman's boy
  That he shouts with his sister at play!
O, well for the sailor lad
  That he sings in his boat on the bay!

And the stately ships go on,
  To the haven under the hill;
But O, for the touch of a vanished hand,
  And the sound of a voice that is still!

Break, break, break,
  At the foot of thy crags, O, sea!
But the tender grace of a day that is dead
  Will never come back to me.

THERE IS NO DEATH.

BY J. L. McCREERY.

This beautifully touching poem is the creation of Mr. J. L. McCreery, a native of Iowa, and at one time editor of the Delaware County Journal, of that state. The poem was written in 1863 and was first published in Arthur's Home Magazine in July of that year. The authorship of the poem was for many years erroneously attributed to Lord Lytton, the English poet. A thorough investigation carried on by Lippincott's a few years ago fully established the authorship. The poem has been printed in every state of the Union, in England, Scotland, Ireland, Wales, Canada, and even in Australia. It has gone into dozens of school books and been incorporated in scores of miscellaneous collections of poetry. It has been quoted in full or in part at least five times on the floor of Congress. Mr. McCreery has for the past few years been a resident of the national capital and his best poems have been collected into a volume entitled "Songs of Toil and Triumph."

There is no death, the stars go down
　　To rise upon some other shore,
And bright in heaven's jeweled crown
　　They shine forever more.

There is no death! the forest leaves
　　Convert to life the viewless air;
The rocks disorganize to feed
　　The hungry moss they bear.

There is no death! the dust we tread
　　Shall change, beneath the summer showers,
To golden grain, or mellow fruit,
　　Or rainbow-tinted flowers.

There is no death! the leaves may fall,
　　The flowers may fade and pass away—
They only wait, through wintry hours,
　　The warm, sweet breath of May.

There is no death! the choicest gifts
    That heaven hath kindly lent to earth
Are ever first to seek again
    The country of their birth.

And all things that for growth of joy
    Are worthy of our love or care,
Whose loss has left us desolate,
    Are safely garnered there.

Though life become a dreary waste,
    We know its fairest, sweetest flowers,
Transplanted into paradise,
    Adorn immortal bowers.

The voice of bird-like melody
    That we have missed and mourned so long
Now mingles with the angel choir
    In everlasting song.

There is no death! although we grieve
    When beautiful, familiar forms
That we have learned to love are torn
    From our embracing arms.

Although with bowed and breaking heart,
    With sable garb and silent tread,
We bear their senseless dust to rest,
    And say that they are "dead."

They are not dead! they have but passed
    Beyond the mists that blind us here
Into the new and larger life
    Of that serener sphere.

They have but dropped their robe of clay
    To put their shining raiment on;
They have not wandered far away—
    They are not "lost" or "gone."

Though disenthralled and glorified,
   They still are here and love us yet;
The dear ones they have left behind
   They never can forget.

And sometimes, when our hearts grow faint
   Amid temptations fierce and deep,
Or when the wildly raging waves
   Of grief or passion sweep,

We feel upon our fevered brow
   Their gentle touch, their breath of balm;
Their arms enfold us, and our hearts
   Grow comforted and calm.

And ever near us, though unseen,
   The dear, immortal spirits tread;
For all the boundless universe
   Is life—there are no dead.

THE FOOL'S PRAYER.
BY E. R. SILL.

Edward Rowland Sill was born at Windsor, Conn., April 29, 1841; died in Cleveland, O., Feb. 27, 1887. He was graduated from Yale in 1861; studied biology at Harvard, did literary work in New York City, taught school in California and Ohio, and was for eight years professor of English language and literature in the University of California. His poems were privately printed under the title "The Hermitage and Other Poems."

The royal feast was done; the king
   Sought some new sport to banish care,
And to his jester cried: "Sir Fool,
   Kneel now, and make for us a prayer!"

The jester doffed his cap and bells,
   And stood the mocking court before;
They could not see the bitter smile
   Behind the painted grin he wore.

He bowed his head, and bent his knee
   Upon the monarch's silken stool;
His pleading voice arose: "O Lord,
   Be merciful to me, a fool!

"No pity, Lord, could change the heart
   From red with wrong to white as wool;
The rod must heal the sin; but, Lord,
   Be merciful to me, a fool!

" 'Tis not by guilt the onward sweep
    Of truth and right, O Lord, we stay;
 'Tis by our follies that so long
    We hold the earth from heaven away.

"These clumsy feet, still in the mire,
    Go crushing blossoms without end;
These hard, well meaning hands we thrust
    Among the heart-strings of a friend.

"The ill-timed truth we might have kept—
    Who knows how sharp it pierced and stung!
The word we had not sense to say—
    Who knows how grandly it had rung!

"Our faults no tenderness should ask,
    The chastening stripes must cleanse them all;
But for our blunders—O, in shame
    Before the eyes of heaven we fall.

"Earth bears no balsam for mistakes;
    Men crown the knave and scourge the tool
That did his will; but thou, O Lord,
    Be merciful to me, a fool!"

The room was hushed; in silence rose
    The king, and sought his gardens cool,
And walked apart, and murmured low,
    "Be merciful to me, a fool!"

ROCK ME TO SLEEP.

BY ELIZABETH AKERS ALLEN.

This is one of the songs which, as Longfellow said, gush from the heart of "some humbler poet." In this country, at least, it has been extremely popular, having been set to music and sung in innumerable households. Elizabeth Akers Allen was born in 1832, and still lives at Tuckahoe, N. Y. She wrote poetry from the age of 15, and has published many volumes. The poem here published first appeared in 1859. A new volume of her verse is just announced in Boston.

Backward, turn backward, O Time in your flight,
Make me a child again just for tonight;
Mother, come back from the echoless shore,
Take me again to your heart as of yore;
Kiss from my forehead the furrows of care,
Smooth the few silver threads out of my hair;
Over my slumbers your loving watch keep;
Rock me to sleep, mother—rock me to sleep.

Backward, flow backward, O tide of the years,
I am so weary of toil and of tears—
Toil without recompense, tears all in vain—
Take them, and give me my childhood again!
I have grown weary of dust and decay—
Weary of flinging my soul-wealth away;
Weary of sowing for others to reap;
Rock me to sleep, mother—rock me to sleep.

Tired of the hollow, the base, the untrue,
Mother, O mother, my heart calls for you!
Many a summer the grass has grown green,
Blossomed, and faded our faces between!

Yet, with strong yearning and passionate pain
Long I tonight for your presence again.
Come from the silence so long and so deep—
Rock me to sleep, mother—rock me to sleep.

Over my heart in the days that are flown
No love like mother love ever has shone;
No other worship abides and endures—
Faithful, unselfish, and patient like yours;
None like a mother can charm away pain
From the sick soul and world weary brain.
Slumber's soft calms o'er the heavy lids creep—
Rock me to sleep, mother—rock me to sleep.

Come, let your brown hair, just lighted with gold,
Fall on your shoulders again as of old;
Let it drop over my forehead tonight,
Shading my faint eyes away from the light;
For with its sunny edged shadows once more
Haply will throng the sweet visions of yore;
Lovingly, softly its bright billows sweep;
Rock me to sleep, mother—rock me to sleep.

Mother, dear mother, the years have been long
Since I last hushed to your lullaby song;
Sing, then, and unto my soul it shall seem
Womanhood's years have been only a dream.
Clasped to your heart in a loving embrace,
With your light lashes just sweeping my face,
Never hereafter to wake or to weep—
Rock me to sleep, mother—rock me to sleep.

THE DESTRUCTION OF SENNACHERIB.

BY LORD BYRON.

Lord Byron was born in London in 1788. His first volume of verses, entitled "Hours of Idleness," was printed in 1807. "Manfred" and "The Lament of Tasso" were written in 1817. From 1818 to his death Byron was occupied on "Don Juan." In 1823 he went to Greece, and with advice and money aided in the Greek struggle for independence. He died in Greece in 1824.

"And it came to pass, that night, that the angel of the Lord went out and smote in the camp of the Assyrians an hundred four score and five thousand; and when they arose early in the morning, behold, they were all dead corpses."—II. Kings, xix., 35.

The Assyrian came down like the wolf on the fold,
And his cohorts were gleaming in purple and gold;
And the sheen of their spears was like stars on the sea,
When the blue wave rolls nightly on deep Galilee.

Like the leaves of the forest when summer is green,
That host with their banners at sunset were seen;
Like the leaves of the forest when autumn hath blown,
That host on the morrow lay wither'd and strown.

For the angel of death spread his wings on the blast,
And breathed in the face of the foe as he pass'd;
And the eyes of the sleepers wax'd deadly and chill,
And their hearts but once heaved—and forever grew still.

And there lay the steed with his nostril all wide,
But through it there roll'd not the breath of his pride;
And the foam of his gasping lay white on the turf,
And cold as the spray of the rock beating surf.

And there lay the rider, distorted and pale,
With the dew on his brow and the rust on his mail;
And the tents were all silent, the banners alone,
The lances unlifted, the trumpet unblown.

And the widows of Ashur are loud in their wail,
And the idols are broke in the temple of Baal;
And the might of the Gentile, unsmote by the sword,
Hath melted like snow in the glance of the Lord!

THE DEATH BED.

BY THOMAS HOOD.

Thomas Hood was born in London in 1799, and early in life turned his attention to literary pursuits. At the age of 22 he became sub-editor of the London Magazine, which gave him acquaintance with all the literary men of the age, and an intimacy with Charles Lamb, which continued until his death. He was a voluminous writer, both in poetry and prose, contributing to various magazines. In 1844 Hood's Magazine was started, for which he furnished most of the material until near his death. His best work was done during his last sickness, when, on a bed of suffering, he contributed to Punch those touching verses which have rendered his name immortal: "The Song of the Shirt" and "The Bridge of Sighs." He died May 3, 1845.

We watched her sleeping through the night,
Her breathing soft and low,
As in her breast the wave of life
Kept surging to and fro.
    So silently we seemed to speak,
    So slowly moved about,
    As we had lent her half our powers
    To eke her being out.
Our very hopes belied our fears,
Our fears our hopes belied,
We thought her dying when she slept,
And sleeping when she died.
    For when the morn came dim and sad,
    And chill with early showers,
    Her quiet eyelids closed, she had
    Another morn than ours.

VIRTUE IMMORTAL.
BY GEORGE HERBERT.

George Herbert was born at Montgomery castle in Wales in 1593. He graduated from Trinity College, Cambridge, and in 1619 he was made a public orator. Charles I., with whom he was in great favor, gave him the rectory of Bemerton, which has the reputation of being the smallest church in England. It was here that Herbert wrote his religious poems, "The Temple: Sacred Poems and Private Ejaculations." He died at Bemerton in 1633.

Sweet day, so cool, so calm, so bright;
    The bridal of the earth and sky;
The dew shall weep thy fall tonight,
    For thou must die.

Sweet rose, whose hue, angry and brave,
    Bids the rash gazer wipe his eye,
Thy root is ever in its grave,
    And thou must die.

Sweet spring, full of sweet days and roses,
    A box where sweets compacted lie,
Thy music shows ye have your closes,
    And all must die.

Only a sweet and virtuous soul,
    Like seasoned timber never gives,
But, though the whole world turn to coal,
    Then chiefly lives.

TO LUCASTA, ON GOING TO THE WARS

BY RICHARD LOVELACE.

Richard Lovelace was an English cavalier, born in 1618, a period which produced many poets. He was educated both at the Charterhouse and at Oxford. He was twice imprisoned on account of the active part he took in the affairs of the times. After the execution of Charles, he was set free from prison only to find that his estates had been confiscated. He died in great poverty in London, in 1658. After his death his poems were collected under the name of "Lucasta, Posthume Poems." The name of the lady to whom the poems were written was Lucy Sacheverell, whom he called his "Lux Castra."

Tell me not, Sweet, I am unkind,
  That from the nunnery
Of thy chaste breast and quiet
      mind,
  To war and arms I fly.

True, a new mistress now I chase,
  The first foe in the field;
And with a stronger faith em -
      brace
  A sword, a horse, a shield.

Yet this inconstancy is such
  As you, too, shall adore;
  I could not love thee, Dear, so
      much,
Loved I not Honor more.

CHERRY RIPE.

BY THOMAS CAMPION.

There is a garden in her face
    Where roses and white lilies blow,
A heavenly paradise is that place,
    Wherein all pleasant fruits do grow;
There cherries grow that none may buy,
Till Cherry-Ripe themselves do cry.

Those cherries fairly do enclose
    Of orient pearl a double row,
Which, when her lovely laughter shows,
    They look like rose-buds fill'd with snow;
Yet them no peer nor prince may buy,
Till Cherry-Ripe themselves do cry.

Her eyes like angels watch them still;
    Her brows like bended bows do stand,
Threat'ning with piercing frowns to kill
    All that approach with eye or hand
These sacred cherries to come nigh,
Till Cherry-Ripe themselves do cry.

TO THINE OWN SELF BE TRUE.

BY PAKENHAM BEATTY.

Pakenham Beatty was born in 1855. He has written several volumes
—"To My Lady," 1878; "Three Women of the People," 1881; and "Mar-
cia, a Tragedy," 1884.

By thine own soul's law learn to live,
    And if men thwart thee take no heed,
And if men hate thee have no care;
    Sing thou thy song and do thy deed.
Hope thou thy hope and pray thy prayer,
    And claim no crown they will not give,
Nor bays they grudge thee for thy hair.

Keep thou thy soul-worn steadfast oath,
    And to thy heart be true thy heart;
What thy soul teaches learn to know,
    And play out thine appointed part,
And thou shalt reap as thou shalt sow,
    Nor helped nor hindered in thy growth,
To thy full stature thou shalt grow.

Fix on the future's goal thy face,
    And let thy feet be lured to stray
Nowhither, but be swift to run,
    And nowhere tarry by the way,
Until at last the end is won
    And thou mayst look back from thy place
And see thy long day's journey done.

O, CAPTAIN! MY CAPTAIN!

BY WALT WHITMAN.

Walt Whitman was born on Long Island, N. Y., in 1819. His father was a carpenter. After the family removed to Brooklyn Walt became apprenticed to a newspaper, and at 12 began to write bits of verse, some of which were published in the New York Mirror. He made a series of long tramping tours through the country, returning finally to newspaper work in Brooklyn. He became known to the public as a poet through his "Leaves of Grass," published in 1885. The volume was declared immoral by some, and the author severely criticised. "Leaves of Grass" has been republished a number of times in the United States, England, and Scotland, and among Whitman's other works are "Drum Taps," "As Strong as a Bird on Pinions Free," "Two Rivulets," "Specimen Days and Collect," "November Boughs," and "Sands at Seventy." He died in 1892.

O, Captain! my Captain! our fearful trip is done,
The ship has weather'd every rack, the prize we sought is won,
The port is near, the bells I hear, the people all exulting,
While follow eyes the steady keel, the vessel grim and daring;

But, O, heart! heart! heart!
O, the bleeding drops of red,
Where on the deck my Captain lies,
Fallen cold and dead.

O, Captain! my Captain! rise up and hear the bells;
Rise up—for you the flag is flung—for you the bugle trills,
For you bouquets and ribbon'd wreaths—for you the shores
a-crowding,
For you they call, the swaying mass, their eager faces turning;

Here, Captain! dear father!
This arm beneath your head!
It is some dream that on the deck,
You've fallen cold and dead.

My Captain does not answer, his lips are pale and still,
My father does not feel my arm, he has no pulse nor will,
His ship is anchor'd safe and sound, its voyage closed and
done,
From fearful trip the victor ship comes in with object won;

Exult, O shores, and ring, O bells!
　　But I with mournful tread,
Walk the deck my Captain lies,
　　Fallen cold and dead.

BABYHOOD.

BY JOSIAH GILBERT HOLLAND.

Josiah Gilbert Holland was born in Belchertown, Mass., July 24, 1819; died in New York City Oct. 12, 1881. He was the son of a mechanic and inventor. He attended a district school, taught district schools, studied medicine, and in 1844 was graduated from the Berkshire medical college, which exists no longer, at Pittsfield. He practiced medicine for three years, ran a weekly paper six months, became superintendent of schools in Vicksburg, Miss., formed a literary, reportorial, and editorial connection with the Springfield Republican in 1850, which lasted until 1866, he having in the meantime acquired a financial interest in the paper. Some of his best works appeared first in the Republican. In 1870, with Roswell Smith, he founded Scribner's Magazine. He wrote histories, stories, essays, letters, lectures, and poems.

What is the little one thinking about?
Very wonderful things, no doubt!
  Unwritten history!
  Unfathomed mystery!
Yet chuckles and crows and nods and winks,
As if his head were as full of kinks
And curious riddles as any sphinx!
  Warped by colic and wet by tears,
  Punctured by pins and tortured by fears
  Our little nephew will lose two years;
   And he'll never know
   Where the summers go—
He need not laugh, for he'll find it so.

Who can tell what a baby thinks?
Who can follow the gossamer links
  By which the manikin feels his way
Out from the shore of the great unknown,
Blind and wailing, and alone,
  Into the light of day?

Out from the shore of the unknown sea,
Tossing in pitiful agony—
Of the unknown sea that reels and rolls,
Specked with the barks of little souls—
Barks that were launched on the other side,
And slipped from heaven on an ebbing tide!

What does he think of his mother's eyes?
    What does he think of his mother's hair?
What of the cradle roof that flies
    Forward and backward through the air?
What does he think of his mother's breast,
    Bare and beautiful, smooth and white,
    Seeking it ever with fresh delight—
        Cup of his life and couch of his rest?
What does he think when her quick embrace
Presses his hand and buries his face
Deep where the heart throbs sink and swell
With a tenderness she can never tell,
    Though she murmur the words
    Of all the birds—
Words she has learned to murmur well?
    Now he thinks he'll go to sleep!
    I can see the shadow creep
    Over his eyes in soft eclipse,
    Over his brow and over his lips,
    Out to his little finger tips!
    Softly sinking, down he goes!
    Down he goes! down he goes!
    See! he is hushed in sweet repose!

EYBUNG
ILLUSTRATION COPYRIGHT 1902
by WELDING COMPANY.

REMEMBRANCE.

BY EMILY BRONTE.

This poem, as well as all of Emily Bronte's verses, is tinged with the deepest melancholy—the sorrow which both Charlotte and Emily Bronte experienced, and which has set them apart in the world of letters from those who do not feel so deeply the emotions of which they write.

Cold in the earth—and the deep snow piled above thee,
　Far, far removed, cold in the dreary grave!
Have I forgot, my only Love, to love thee,
　Sever'd at last by Time's all severing wave?

Now, when alone, do my thoughts no longer hover
　Over the mountains, on that northern shore,
Resting their wings where heath and fern leaves cover
　Thy noble heart for ever, ever more?

Sweet love of youth, forgive, if I forget thee,
   While the world's tide is bearing me along;
Other desires and other hopes beset me,
   Hopes which obscure, but cannot do thee wrong!

No later light has lighten'd up my heaven,
   No second morn has ever shown for me;
All my life's bliss from thy dear life was given,
   All my life's bliss is in the grave with thee.

But when the days of golden dreams had perish'd,
   And even despair was powerless to destroy;
Then did I learn how existence could be cherish'd
   Strengthen'd, and fed without the aid of joy.

Then did I check the tears of useless passion—
   Wean'd my young soul from yearning after thine;
Sternly denied its burning wish to hasten
   Down to that tomb already more than mine.

And, even yet, I dare not let it languish,
   Dare not indulge in memory's rapturous pain;
Once drinking deep of that divinest anguish,
   How could I seek the empty world again?

PSALM XLVI.

God is our refuge and strength,
A very present help in trouble,
Therefore will not we fear, though the earth be removed,
And though the mountains be carried into the midst of the sea;
Though the waters thereof roar and be troubled,
Though the mountains shake with the swelling thereof,
There is a river, the streams whereof shall make glad the city
      of God,
The holy place of the tabernacles of the most High.
God is in the midst of her; she shall not be moved;
God shall help her, and that right early.
The heathen raged, the kingdoms were moved;
He uttered his voice, the earth melted.
The Lord of Hosts is with us;
The God of Jacob is our refuge.
Come, behold the works of the Lord,
What desolations he hath made in the earth,
He maketh wars to cease unto the end of the earth;
He breaketh the bow, and cutteth the spear in sunder;
He burneth the chariot in the fire.
Be still and know that I am God;
I will be exalted among the heathen,
I will be exalted in the earth.
The Lord of Hosts is with us;
The God of Jacob is our refuge.

FOR ALL THESE.

BY JULIET WILBOR TOMPKINS.

I thank thee, Lord, that I am straight and strong,
  With wit to work and hope to keep me brave;
That two score years, unfathomed, still belong
  To the allotted life thy bounty gave.

I thank thee that the sight of sunlit lands
  And dipping hills, the breath of evening grass—
That wet, dark rocks and flowers in my hands
  Can give me daily gladness as I pass.

I thank thee that I love the things of earth—
  Ripe fruits and laughter lying down to sleep,
The shine of lighted towns, the graver worth
  Of beating human hearts that laugh and weep.

I thank thee that as yet I need not know,
  Yet need not fear, the mystery of the end;
But more than all, and though all these should go—
  Dear Lord, this on my knees!—I thank thee for my friend.

RUTHLESS TIME.

BY WILLIAM SHAKSPEARE.
(From "Troilus and Cressida.")

Time hath, my lord, a wallet at his back,
Wherein he puts alms for oblivion,
A great sized monster of ingratitudes;
Those scraps are good deeds past; which are devour'd
As fast as they are made, forgot as soon
As done: perseverance, dear my lord,
Keeps honor bright; to have done is to hang
Quite out of fashion, like a rusty mail
In monumental mockery. Take th' instant way;
For honor travels in a straight so narrow,
Where one but goes abreast; keep, then, the path;
For emulation hath a thousand sons,
That one by one pursue: if you give way,
Or hedge aside from the direct forthright,
Like to an enter'd tide, they all rush by
And leave you hindmost;
Or like a gallant horse fallen in first rank,
Lie there for pavement to the abject rear,
O'errun and trampled on.

A DEED AND A WORD.

BY CHARLES MACKAY.

Charles Mackay was born at Perth in 1814. He was, from 1844 to 1847, the editor of the Glasgow Argus, and later of the Illustrated London News. During the civil war he was the New York correspondent for the London Times. He died at London in 1889. Several of his writings are "The Salamandrine, or Love and Immortality," "Voices from the Crowd," "Voices from the Mountains," and "History of the Mormons."

A little stream had lost its way
   Amid the grass and fern;
A passing stranger scooped a well,
   Where weary men might turn;
He walled it in, and hung with care
   A ladle at the brink;
He thought not of the deed he did,
   But judged that all might drink.

He passed again, and lo! the well,
   By summer never dried,
Had cooled ten thousand parching tongues,
   And saved a life beside.

A nameless man, amid a crowd
   That thronged the daily mart,
Let fall a word of hope and love,
   Unstudied, from the heart;
A whisper on the tumult thrown,
   A transitory breath—
It raised a brother from the dust,
   It saved a soul from death.
O germ! O fount! O word of love!
   O thought at random cast!
Ye were but little at the first,
   But mighty at the last.

TWO LOVERS.

BY GEORGE ELIOT.

Mary Ann Evans was born at Warwickshire, in 1819. She received her education at Nuneaton, and also at Coventry. In 1851 she was given the position of assistant editor on the "Westminster Review," which she held until 1853. In the following year she entered into a domestic and philosophical partnership with George Henry Lewes. Two years after his death she married John Walter Cross, a man much younger than herself. After her death her husband published her memoirs. She died at Chelsea, London, in 1880. Though shunned by the women of her acquaintance, Eliot was courted by the greatest philosophers of her time.

Two lovers by a moss-grown spring:
They leaned soft cheeks together there,
Mingled the dark and sunny hair,
And heard the wooing thrushes sing.
     O budding time!
     O love's blest prime!

Two wedded from the portal stept:
The bells made happy carolings,
The air was soft as fanning wings,
White petals on the pathway slept.
    O pure-eyed bride!
    O tender pride!

Two faces o'er a cradle bent:
Two hands above the head were locked;
These pressed each other while they rocked,
Those watched a life that love had sent.
    O solemn hour!
    O hidden power!

Two parents by the evening fire:
The red light fell about their knees
On heads that rose by slow degrees
Like buds upon the lily spire.
    O patient life!
    O tender strife!

The two still sat together there,
The red light shone about their knees;
But all the heads by slow degrees
Had gone and left that lonely pair.
    O voyage fast!
    O vanished past!

The red light shone upon the floor
And made the space between them wide;
They drew their chairs up side by side,
Their pale cheeks joined, and said,
    "Once more!"
    O memories!
    O past that is!

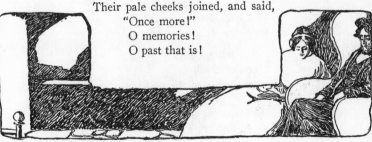

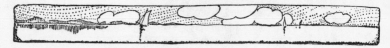

DRIFTING.

BY THOMAS BUCHANAN READ.

Thomas Buchanan Read, artist and poet, was born in 1822 and died in 1872. His youth was spent in poverty and he earned a miserable existence at tailoring and cigarmaking. He played on the stage and took to painting in oils. His work attracted interest and he opened a studio. About the same time he began writing, alternating the brush with the pen. His best-known poems are "Sheridan's Ride" and "Drifting." He published a volume of poetry and two of prose. His pictures include portraits of Longfellow, Dallas, Ex-Queen of Naples, Mrs. Browning and "The Lost Pleiad," "The Star of Bethlehem," "Spirit of the Waterfall," and "Sheridan's Ride."

My soul today
Is far away,
Sailing the Vesuvian Bay;
My winged boat,
A bird afloat,
Swims round the purple peaks remote:—

Round purple peaks
It sails, and seeks
Blue inlets and their crystal creeks,
Where high rocks throw,
Through deeps below,
A duplicated golden glow.

Far, vague, and dim,
The mountains swim;
While on Vesuvius' misty brim
With outstretched hands
The gray smoke stands
O'erlooking the volcanic lands.

Here Ischia smiles
O'er liquid miles;
And yonder, bluest of the isles,
Calm Capri waits,
Her sapphire gates
Beguiling to her bright estates.

I heed not, if
My rippling skiff
Float swift or slow from cliff to cliff;—
With dreamful eyes
My spirit lies
Under the walls of Paradise.

Under the walls
Where swells and falls
The bay's deep breast at intervals,
At peace I lie,
Blown softly by,
A cloud upon this liquid sky.

The day so mild,
Is Heaven's own child,
With earth and ocean reconciled;—
The airs I feel
Around me steal
Are murmuring to the murmuring keel.

Over the rail
My hand I trail
Within the shadow of the sail.
A joy intense,
The cooling sense
Glides down my drowsy indolence.

With dreamful eyes
My spirit lies
Where summer sings and never dies,—
O'erveiled with vines.
She glows and shines
Among her future oil and wines.

Her children hid,
The cliffs amid,
Are gamboling with the gamboling kid;
Or down the walls,
With tipsy calls,
Laugh on the rocks like waterfalls.

The fisher's child
With tresses wild,
Unto the smooth, bright sand beguiled,
With glowing lips,
Sings as she skips,
Or gazes at the far-off ships.

Yon deep bark goes
Where Traffic blows,
From lands of sun to lands of snows;—
This happier one
Its course has run
From lands of snow to lands of sun.

O happy ship,
To rise and dip,
With the blue crystal at your lip!
O happy crew,
My heart with you
Sails, and sails, and sings anew!

No more, no more
The worldy shore
Upbraids me with its loud uproar!
With dreamful eyes
My spirit lies
Under the walls of Paradise!

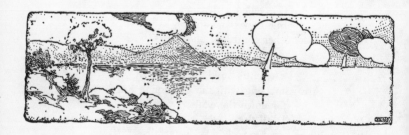

DIRGE FOR A SOLDIER.

BY GEORGE H. BOKER.

George Henry Boker, the American poet, was born in Philadelphia
in 1823, and died there in 1890. He was educated at Princeton, and
studied law, but never practiced. In 1871 he was made Minister Resident to Turkey, and from 1875 to 1879 he was Minister to Russia. He
wrote several volumes of verse and the tragedies "Francesca da
Rimini," "Anne Boleyn," and "Leonore de Guzman."

Close his eyes; his work is done!
    What to him is friend or foeman,
Rise of moon or set of sun,
    Hand of man or kiss of woman?
    Lay him low, lay him low,
    In the clover or the snow!
    What cares he? He cannot know;
      Lay him low!

As man may, he fought his fight,
    Proved his truth by his endeavor;
Let him sleep in solemn might,
    Sleep for ever and forever.
    Lay him low, lay him low,
    In the clover or the snow!
    What cares he? He cannot know;
      Lay him low!

Fold him in his country's stars,
    Roll the drum and fire the volley!
What to him are all our wars,
    What but death bemocking folly?
    Lay him low, lay him low
      In the clover or the snow!
      What cares he? He cannot know;
        Lay him low!

    Leave him to God's watching eye;
      Trust him to the hand that made him.
    Mortal love weeps idly by;
      God alone has power to aid him.
      Lay him low, lay him low,
      In the clover or the snow!
      What cares he? He cannot know;
        Lay him low!

EVENING SONG.

BY SIDNEY LANIER.

Sidney Lanier was born at Macon, Ga., in 1842. On account of ill health he went to Baltimore, where for a while he played the flute in the famous Peabody concerts—he was passionately fond of music and brought marvelous harmonies out of his flute. In 1879 he became lecturer in English literature at the Johns Hopkins university, Baltimore. He died at Lynn, N. C., in 1881. He wrote a novel, "Tiger Lilies," "Centennial Ode," "Science of English Verse," "The English Novel and Its Development," and a volume of poems.

Look off, dear love, across the sallow sands,
   And mark yon meeting of the sun and sea,
How long they kiss in sight of all the lands,
   Ah! longer, longer, we.

Now in the sea's red vintage melts the sun,
   As Egypt's pearl dissolved in rosy wine,
And Cleopatra night drinks all. 'Tis done,
   Love, lay thy hand in mine.

Come forth, sweet stars, and comfort heaven's heart;
   Glimmer, ye waves, round else unlighted sands.
O, night! divorce our sun and sky apart,
   Never our lips our hands.

THE BRIDGE.

BY HENRY WADSWORTH LONGFELLOW.

The poems of this well-loved poet are the stepping stones by which
every American child ascends to the realm of poetry.

I stood on the bridge at midnight,
　As the clocks were striking the hour,
And the moon rose o'er the city
　Behind the dark church tower.

I saw her bright reflection
　In the waters under me,
Like a golden goblet falling
　And sinking into the sea.

And far in the hazy distance
　Of that lovely night in June
The blaze of the flaming furnace
　Gleamed redder than the moon.

Among the long, black rafters
　The wavering shadows lay,
And the current that came from the ocean
　Seemed to lift and bear them away;

As, sweeping and eddying through them,
　Rose the belated tide,
And, streaming into the moonlight,
　The seaweed floated wide.

And like those waters rushing
  Among the wooden piers,
A flood of thoughts came o'er me
  That filled my eyes with tears.

How often, O, how often,
  In the days that had gone by,
I had stood on that bridge at midnight
  And gazed on that wave and sky!

How often, O, how often,
  I had wished that the ebbing tide
Would bear me away on its bosom
  O'er the ocean wild and wide!

For my heart was hot and restless,
  And my life was full of care,
And the burden laid upon me
  Seemed greater than I could bear.

But now it has fallen from me—
  It is buried in the sea;
And only the sorrow of others
  Throws its shadow over me.

Yet whenever I cross the river
  On its bridge with wooden piers,
Like the odor of brine from the ocean
  Comes the thought of other years.

And I think how many thousands
  Of care-encumbered men,
Each bearing his burden of sorrow,
  Have crossed the bridge since then.

I see the long procession
  Still passing to and fro—
The young heart hot and restless,
  And the old subdued and slow!

And forever and forever,
   As long as the river flows,
As long as the heart has passions,
   As long as life has woes,

The moon and its broken reflection
   And its shadow shall appear,
As the symbol of love in heaven,
   And its wavering image here.

SHE WALKS IN BEAUTY, LIKE THE NIGHT.
BY LORD BYRON.

She walks in beauty, like the night
   Of cloudless climes and starry skies,
And all that's best of dark and bright
   Meet in her aspect and her eyes,
Thus mellow'd to that tender light
   Which heaven to gaudy day denies.

One shade the more, one ray the less
   Had half impaired the nameless grace
Which waves in every raven tress
   Or softly lightens o'er her face,
Where thoughts serenely sweet express
   How pure, how dear their dwelling place.

And on that cheek and o'er that brow,
   So soft, so calm, yet eloquent,
The smiles that win, the tints that glow
   But tell of days in goodness spent—
A mind at peace with all below,
   A heart whose love is innocent.

THE SPACIOUS FIRMAMENT ON HIGH.

BY JOSEPH ADDISON.

Joseph Addison was born at Milston in 1672. He went to Queen's College, Oxford; after he finished his course he traveled on the continent, studying for the diplomatic service. Returning, he held the position of Secretary of State, 1706-'8, and until a year of his death held different political positions. He wrote, besides his famous contributions to the Tatler, and Spectator, "The Campaign," a treatise on Medals, a "Letter from Italy," and one play worthy the name, "Cato." He died at London in 1719.

The spacious firmament on high,
With all the blue ethereal sky,
And spangled heavens a shining frame,
Their great Original proclaim.
The unwearied sun, from day to day,
Does his Creator's power display,
And publishes to every land
The work of an Almighty hand.

Soon as the evening shades prevail
The moon takes up the wondrous tale,
And nightly to the listening earth
Repeats the story of her birth;
Whilst all the stars that round her burn,
And all the planets in their turn
Confirm the tidings as they roll,
And spread the truth from pole to pole.

What though in solemn silence all
Move round the dark terrestrial ball;
What though no real voice nor sound
Amidst their radiant orbs be found;
In reason's ear they all rejoice
And utter forth a glorious voice;
Forever singing, as they shine,
"The hand that made us is divine."

LUCY.

BY WILLIAM WORDSWORTH.

She dwelt among the untrodden ways
   Beside the springs of Dove;
A maid whom there were none to praise,
   And very few to love.

A violet by a mossy stone
   Half hidden from the eye!
Fair as a star, when only one
   Is shining in the sky.

She lived unknown and few could know
   When Lucy ceased to be;
But she is in her grave, and, O,
   The difference to me!

AN EMPEROR'S DAUGHTER STANDS ALONE.

BY GEOFFREY CHAUCER.

Geoffrey Chaucer, often called the father of English verse, was born some time after 1340, served with Edward III. in the French campaigns and was imprisoned in France. He was on an embassy to Genoa in 1372, met Petrarch, and got from him the tale of Griselda and other Italian legends. On his return he occupied various positions of trust, principally of a diplomatic nature. His last days were spent in obscurity. He died in London in 1400, and was buried in Westminster Abbey. His "Canterbury Tales," founded for the most part upon the same stories that Boccaccio and other writers had made famous in prose, are almost the first evidence of the influence of the Italian Renaissance upon English literature. He wrote many detached pieces as well, although his reputation rests largely upon the "Tales." He had not only the true poetic instinct, but a deep knowledge and intense love of nature, and he gave a great inspiration to the writers of the golden age which followed his own. As Tennyson says of him in "A Dream of Fair Women:"

> "Dan Chaucer, the first warbler whose sweet breath
> Preluded those melodious bursts that fill
> The spacious times of great Elizabeth
> With sounds that echo still."

Have ye nat seyn som tyme a pale face
Among a press, of hym that hath be lad
Toward his deeth, where as hym gat no grace?
And swich a colour in his face hath had,
Men myghte knowe his face that was bistad,
Amonges alle the faces in that route;
So stant Custance, and looketh hire aboute.

   O, queenes, lyvynge in prosperitee!
Duchesses, and ladyes everichone!
Haveth som routhe on hire adversitee.
An Emperoures doghter stant allone;
She hath no wight to whom to make hir mone!
O, blood roial, that stondest in this drede,

Fer been thy freendes at thy grete nede!
This Alla, kyng, hath swich compassioun,
As gentil herte is fulfild of pitee,
That from hise eyen ran the water doun.
"Now hastily do fecche a book," quod he,
"And if this knyght wol sweren how that she
This womman slow, yet wol we us avyse
Whom that we wole that shall been our justise."

A Briton book written with Evaungiles
Was fet, and on this book he swore anoon
She gilty was, and in the meene whiles
An hand hym smoot upon the nekke boon,
That doun he fil atones as a stoon;
And bothe hise eyen broste out of his face
In sighte of every body in that place!

A voys was herd in general audience
And seyde, "Thou has desclaundred, giltlees,
The doghter of hooly chirche in heigh presence;
Thus hastou doon, and yet holde I my pees."
Of this mervaille agast was al the prees;
As mazed folk they stoden everichone,
For drede of wreche, save Custance allone.

Greet was the drede, and eek the repentance,
Of hem that hadden wronge suspecioun
Upon this sely, innocent Custance;
And for this miracle, in conclusion,
And by Custance's mediacioun,
The Kyng, and many another in that place
Converted was—thanked be Christes grace!

DELIGHT IN DISORDER.

BY ROBERT HERRICK.

It is in such poems as the following one that Herrick is at his best; his religious, or, as he called them, his "noble numbers," being for the most part inferior. But in his lyrics, as Austin Dobson says, his "numbers are of gold."

A sweet disorder in the dress
Kindles in clothes a wantonness;
A lawn about the shoulders thrown,
Into a fine distraction;
An erring lace, which here and there
Enthralls the crimson stomacher;
A cuff neglected, and thereby
Ribbands to flow confusedly;
A winning wave, deserving note,
In the tempestuous petticoat;
A careless shoestring, in whose tie
I see a wild civility;
Doth more bewitch me than when art
Is too precise in every part.

OFT IN THE STILLY NIGHT.

BY THOMAS MOORE.

Oft in the stilly night,
  E're slumber's chain has bound me,
Fond Memory brings the light
  Of another day around me:
    The smiles, the tears,
    Of boyhood's years,
The words of love then spoken;
  The eyes that shone
  Now dimmed and gone,
The cheerful hearts now broken.

When I remember all
  The friends so linked together,
I've seen around me fall,
  Like leaves in wintry weather,
    I feel like one
    Who treads alone
Some banquet hall deserted,
    Whose lights are fled,
    Whose garlands dead,
And all but he departed.

  Thus in the stilly night,
    E're slumber's chain has bound me,
  Sad Memory brings the light
    Of other days around me.

JIM BLUDSO.

JOHN HAY.

John Hay, Secretary of State, was born at Salem, Ind., on Oct. 8, 1838, and he was graduated at Brown twenty years later. He studied law in Springfield, Ill., and in 1861 became assistant secretary to President Lincoln. He saw some of the civil war as an aid-de-camp under Generals Hunter and Gilmore, with rank of Major and Assistant Adjutant General, Brevet Lieutenant Colonel and Colonel. He was First Assistant Secretary of Legation in Paris and in charge several times from 1865 to 1867, was diplomat in charge at Vienna 1867-'68, Secretary of Legation at Madrid 1868-'70, editorial writer for five years of the New York Tribune, First Assistant Secretary of State, and Ambassador to England. He is the author of "Pike County Ballads," "Castillian Days," and part author of a life of Lincoln, written in conjunction with John G. Nicolay.

Wall no! I can't tell where he lives
    Because he don't live, you see;
Leastways he's got out of the habit
    Of livin' like you and me.
Whar have you been for the last three years,
    That you haven't heard folks tell
How Jimmy Bludso passed in his checks
    The night of the Prairie Belle?

He weren't no saint—them engineers
    Is all pretty much alike—
One wife in Natchez-Under-the-Hill
    And another one here in Pike;
A keerless man in his talk was Jim,
    And an awkward man in a row,
But he never flunked and he never lied—
    I reckon he never knowed how.

And this was all the religion he had—
    To treat his engine well;
Never be passed on the river;
    To mind the pilot's bell;

And if ever the Prairie Belle took fire—
  A thousand times he swore
He'd hold her nozzle agin the bank
  Till the last soul got ashore.

All boats has their day on the Mississipp,
  And her day come at last—
The Movastar was a better boat,
  But the Belle she wouldn't be passed,
And so she come tearin' along that night—
  The oldest craft on the line—
With a nigger squat on her safety-valve
  And her furnace crammed, rosin and pine.

The fire bust out as she clared the bar,
  And burnt a hole in the night,
And quick as a flash she turned, and made
  For that willer bank on the right.
There was runnin' and cursin', but Jim yelled out,
  Over all the infernal roar,
"I'll hold her nozzle agin the bank
  Till the last galoot's ashore."

Through the hot, black breath of the burnin' boat
  Jim Bludso's voice was heard,
And they all had trust in his cussedness,
  And know'd he would keep his word,
And, sure's you're born they all got off
  Afore the smokestacks fell—
And Bludso's ghost went up alone
  In the smoke of the Prairie Belle.

He weren't no saint—but at jedgment
  I'd run my chance with Jim,
'Longside of some pious gentlemen
  That wouldn't shook hands with him.
He seen his duty, a dead-sure thing—
  And went for it thar and then;
And Christ ain't a-going to be too hard
  On a man that died for men.

MORAL.

BY ALFRED TENNYSON.

So, Lady Flora, take my lay,
　　And if you find no moral there,
Go, look in any glass and say,
　　What moral is in being fair.
Oh, to what uses shall we put
　　The wildweed-flower that simply blows?
And is there any moral shut
　　Within the bosom of the rose?

But any man that walks the mead,
　　In bud or blade, or bloom, may find,
According as his humors lead,
　　A meaning suited to his mind.
And liberal applications lie
　　In Art like Nature, dearest friend;
So 'twere to cramp its use, if I
　　Should hook it to some useful end.

66

BEDOUIN LOVE SONG.
BY BAYARD TAYLOR.

From the desert I come to thee
  On a stallion shod with fire,
And the winds are left behind
  In the speed of my desire.
Under thy window I stand,
  And the midnight hears my cry:
I love thee, I love but thee,
  With a love that shall not die
    Till the sun grows cold,
    And the stars are old,
    And the leaves of the Judgment
    Book unfold!

Look from thy window and see
  My passion and my pain;
I lie on the sands below,
  And I faint in thy disdain.
Let the night winds touch thy brow
  With the heat of my burning sigh,
And melt thee to hear the vow
  Of a love that shall not die
    Till the sun grows cold,
    And the stars are old,
    And the leaves of the Judgment
    Book unfold!

My steps are nightly driven,
  By the fever in my breast,
To hear from thy lattice breathed
  The word that shall give me rest.
Open the door of thy heart,
  And open thy chamber door,

And my kisses shall teach thy lips
  The love that shall fade no more
    Till the sun grows cold,
    And the stars are old,
    And the leaves of the Judgment Book un-
      fold!

SALLY IN OUR ALLEY.

BY HENRY CAREY.

Little is known of this English poet and musical composer except
that he was born near the end of the seventeenth century—about 1693—
and that he is supposed to have committed suicide at London in 1743.
He wrote several burlesques and farces, but is chiefly noted as the
author of "God Save the King" and "Sally in Our Alley."

Of all the girls that are so smart
  There's none like pretty Sally;
She is the darling of my heart,
  And she lives in our alley.
There is no lady in the land
  Is half so sweet as Sally;
She is the darling of my heart,
  And she lives in our alley.

Her father he makes cabbage nets,
  And through the streets does cry 'em;
Her mother she sells laces long
  To such as please to buy 'em;
But sure such folks could ne'er beget
  So sweet a girl as Sally!
She is the darling of my heart,
  And she lives in our alley.

Of all the days that's in the week
  I dearly love but one day—
And that's the day that comes betwixt
  A Saturday and Monday;
For then I'm drest all in my best
  To walk abroad with Sally;
She is the darling of my heart,
  And she lives in our alley.

My master carries me to church,
    And often am I blamed
Because I leave him in the lurch
    As soon as text is named;
I leave the church in sermon time
    And slink away to Sally;
She is the darling of my heart,
    And she lives in our alley.

ELIA.

BY E. J. McPHELIM.

Edward J. McPhelim, a singer of many sweet songs, became mute in 1896 at an age all too young. For several years he was dramatic and literary critic for "The Tribune," departments in which his rare critical ability and wonderful command of language found full scope. His poems, which have never been collected, contain fancies as poetic and delicate as any in the English tongue. The following, on Lamb and his sister, is significant, considering where McPhelim's last days were spent:

Across the English meadows sweet,
    Across the smiling sunset land,
I see them walk with faltering feet,
    Brother and sister, hand in hand.

They know the hour of parting nigh,
    They pass into the dying day,
And, lo! against the sunset sky
    Looms up the madhouse gaunt and gray.

He keeps the lonely lamp aglow,
  While old loves whisper in the air
Of unforgotten long ago
  Before his heart had known despair.

He waits till she may come once more
  From out the darkness to his side,
To share the changeless love of yore
  When all the old, old loves have died.

Between me and this gentle book,
  Shining with humor rich and quaint,
The sad scene rises, and I look
  Upon a jester—or a saint.

I lift my eyes, still brimming o'er
  With love and laughter—and there falls
Across the page forever more,
  The shadow of the madhouse walls!

SONG.

BY WILLIAM SHAKSPEARE.

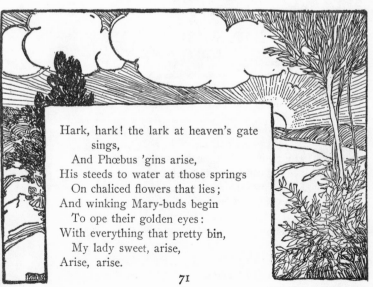

Hark, hark! the lark at heaven's gate
    sings,
  And Phœbus 'gins arise,
His steeds to water at those springs
  On chaliced flowers that lies;
And winking Mary-buds begin
  To ope their golden eyes:
With everything that pretty bin,
  My lady sweet, arise,
Arise, arise.

71

LEAD, KINDLY LIGHT.

BY CARDINAL NEWMAN.

Cardinal Newman was born in London in 1801 and died in 1890. He graduated from Oxford, and was ordained in 1824. He was the recognized leader of the high church party in England until 1845, when he united with the Roman Catholic Church. He was appointed rector of the Catholic university at Dublin in 1854, and was made a Cardinal by the Pope in 1879.

Lead, kindly Light amid the encircling gloom,
    Lead Thou me on!
The night is dark, and I am far from home,
    Lead Thou me on!
Keep Thou my feet! I do not ask to see
The distant scene; one step enough for me.

I was not ever thus, nor prayed that Thou
    Should'st lead me on;
I loved to choose and see my path; but now
    Lead Thou me on!

I loved the garish day; and, spite of fears,
Pride ruled my will; remember not past years.

So long Thy power has blest me, sure it still
    Will lead me on.
O'er moor and fen, o'er crag and torrent, till
    The night is gone;
And with the morn those angel faces smile,
Which I have loved long since, and lost awhile.

AN UNTIMELY THOUGHT.

BY THOMAS BAILEY ALDRICH.

I wonder what day of the week,
    I wonder what month of the year—
Will it be midnight, or morning,
    And who will bend over my bier?

What a hideous fancy to come
    As I wait at the foot of the stair,
While she gives the last touch to her robe
    Or sets the white rose in her hair.

As the carriage rolls down the dark street
    The little wife laughs and makes cheer—
But . . . I wonder what day of the week,
    I wonder what month of the year.

73

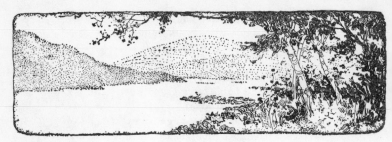

PSALM XIX.

The heavens declare the glory of God; and the firmament sheweth his handiwork.

Day unto day uttereth speech, and night unto night sheweth knowledge.

There is no speech nor language, where their voice is not heard.

Their line is gone out through all the earth, and their words to the end of the world. In them hath he set a tabernacle for the sun.

Which is as a bridegroom coming out of his chamber and rejoiceth as a strong man to run a race.

His going forth is from the end of the heaven, and his circuit unto the ends of it; and there is nothing hid from the heat thereof.

The law of the Lord is perfect, converting the soul: the testimony of the Lord is sure, making wise the simple.

The statutes of the Lord are right, rejoicing the heart: the commandment of the Lord is pure, enlightening the eyes.

The fear of the Lord is clean, enduring forever: the judgments of the Lord are true and righteous altogether.

More to be desired are they than gold, yea, than much fine gold; sweeter also than honey and the honeycomb.

Moreover, by them is thy servant warned: and in keeping of them there is great reward.

Who can understand his errors? Cleanse thou me from secret faults.

Keep back thy servant also from presumptuous sins; let them not have dominion over me: then shall I be upright, and I shall be innocent from the great transgression.

Let the words of my mouth and the meditation of my heart be acceptable in thy sight, O Lord, my strength and my redeemer.

THE POMPADOUR'S FAN.

BY AUSTIN DOBSON.

Austin Dobson is today, as he has been for years, one of the leading English critics and writers of light verse. He is an authority on the literature and society of the sixteenth, seventeenth, and eighteenth centuries, and he excels in verse of the sort here printed.

Chicken-skin, delicate, white,
　　Painted by Carlo Vanloo,
Loves in a riot of light,
　　Roses and vaporous blue;
Hark to the dainty frou-frou!
　　Picture above, if you can,
Eyes that could melt as the dew—
　　This was the Pompadour's fan

See how they rise at the sight,
  Thronging the Oeil de Boeuf through;
Courtiers as butterflies bright,
  Beauties that Fragonard drew,
Talon-rouge, falbala, queue,
  Cardinal, Duke—to a man,
Eager to sigh or to sue—
  This was the Pompadour's fan!

Ah, but things more than polite
  Hung on this toy, voyez-vous!
Matters of state and of might,
  Things that great ministers do;
Things that, may be, overthrew
  Those in whose brains they began;
Here was the sigh and the cue—
  This was the Pompadour's fan!

ENVOY

Where are the secrets it knew?
  Weavings of plot and of plan?
But where is the Pompadour, too?
  This was the Pompadour's fan!

THE BANKS O' DOON.

BY ROBERT BURNS.

Ye banks and braes o' bonnie Doon,
How can ye bloom sae fresh and fair;
How can ye chant, ye little birds,
And I sae weary, fu' o' care!
Thou'lt break my heart, thou warbling bird,
That wantons thro' the flowering thorn;
Thou minds me o' departed joys,
Departed—never to return!

Aft hae I rov'd by bonnie Doon,
To see the rose and woodbine twine;
And ilka bird sang o' its luve,
And fondly sae did I o' mine.
Wi' lightsome heart I pu'd a rose,
Fu' sweet upon its thorny tree;
And my fause luver stole my rose,
But, ah! he left the thorn wi' me.

BALLADE OF NICOLETE.

BY GRAHAM R. TOMSON.

This ballad by a poet of our own time finds its way into the hearts of those who have read and loved the song-story of Aucassin and Nicolete. It has about it the fragrance and naivete of that "good lay," it contains the "force and freshness of young passion, the troubadour's sweetness of literary manner," as Mr. Le Gallienne says of another poem on the same subject written by Edmund Clarence Stedman.

All bathed in pearl and amber light
   She rose to fling the lattice wide,
And leaned into the fragrant night,
   Where brown birds sang of summertide;
('Twas Love's own voice that called and cried)
   "Ah Sweet!" she said, "I'll seek thee yet,
Though thorniest pathways should betide
   The fair white feet of Nicolete."

They slept, who would have staid her flight;
   (Full fain were they the maid had died);
She dropped adown her prison's height
   On strands of linen featly tied.
And so she passed the garden side
   With loose leaved roses sweetly set,
And dainty daisies, dark beside
   The fair white feet of Nicolete!

Her lover lay in evil plight
   (So many lovers yet abide!)
I would my tongue could praise aright
   Her name, that should be glorified.
Those lovers now, whom foes divide
   A little weep—and soon forget.
How far from these faint lovers glide
   The fair white feet of Nicolete.

ENVOY.

My princess, doff thy frozen pride,
   Nor scorn to pay Love's golden debt,
Through his dim woodland take for guide
   The fair white feet of Nicolete.

NIGHT.

BY JOSEPH BLANCO WHITE.

Joseph Blanco White was born of Irish parents in Seville, Spain, July 11, 1775, and was put in training for a mercantile career, but he left his father's counting house and was ordained a priest in 1796, and continued in the priesthood until 1810, when, because of the political crisis in Spain, he went to England, residing in London as a man of letters, where he contributed largely to the leading reviews and periodicals, and produced several books, treating mostly of Spain and its affairs. He died in May, 1841. His "Sonnet to Night" was pronounced by Coleridge the finest in the English language.

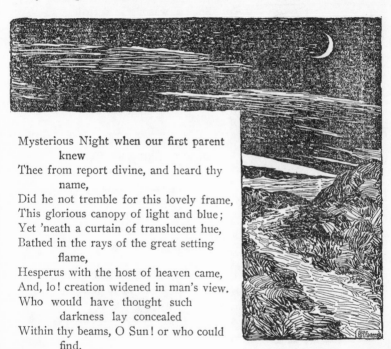

Mysterious Night when our first parent
    knew
Thee from report divine, and heard thy
    name,
Did he not tremble for this lovely frame,
This glorious canopy of light and blue;
Yet 'neath a curtain of translucent hue,
Bathed in the rays of the great setting
    flame,
Hesperus with the host of heaven came,
And, lo! creation widened in man's view.
Who would have thought such
    darkness lay concealed
Within thy beams, O Sun! or who could
    find,
Whilst flower and leaf and insect stood
    revealed,
  That to such countless orbs thou mad'st us blind?
  Why do we then shun death with anxious strife—
  If light can thus deceive us, wherefore not life?

THE SHEPHERD'S RESOLUTION.

BY GEORGE WITHER.

George Wither was born at Brentworth, 1588. He went to Magdalene College, Oxford. He led a troop of Royalist horse against the Covenanters, but three years later he became a Puritan and held command in Cromwell's army. He was imprisoned during the Restoration for a time. He died in 1667. Wither wrote, besides his poems, a volume of church hymns, several satires, and a translation of the Psalms.

Shall I, wasting in despair,
Die because a woman's fair?
Or make pale my cheek with care
'Cause another's rosy are?
Be she fairer than the day,
Or the flow'ry meads in May,
If she be not so to me,
What care I how fair she be?

Shall a woman's virtues move
Me to perish for her love?
Or her well-deservings known
Make me quite forget my own?
Be she with that goodness blest
Which may merit name of best,
If she be not such to me,
What care I how good she be?

Great, or good, or kind, or fair,
I will ne'er the more despair;
If she love me, this believe,
I will die ere she shall grieve;

If she slight me when I woo
I can scorn and let her go,
For if she be not for me,
What care I for whom she be?

THE SONG OF THE MYSTIC.

BY FATHER RYAN.

Father Abram Ryan was born about 1834 some say, in Limerick, Ireland, and others, Norfolk, Va., while still others say, Hagerstown, Md. He lived nearly all his life in the South. He was educated at a seminary at Niagara, N. Y., was ordained to the priesthood and labored in many Southern cities. He established a Catholic newspaper at Augusta, Ga. He died in 1883. He was devoted to the cause of the South, and, aside from his devotional poems, none of his writings have more passion or sincerity than those commemorating the deeds of the Confederate army and the cause for which it fought.

I walk down the Valley of Silence—
　　Down the dim, voiceless valley—alone!
And I hear not the fall of a footstep
　　Around me, save God's and my own;
And the hush of my heart is as holy
　　As hovers where angels have flown!

Long ago I was weary of voices
  Whose music my heart could not win;
Long ago I was weary of noises
  That fretted my soul with their din;
Long ago I was weary of places
  Where I met but the human—and sin.

    *   *   *   *   *   *

In the hush of the Valley of Silence
  I dream all the songs that I sing;
And the music floats down the dim Valley,
  Till each finds a word for a wing,
That to hearts, like the Dove of the Deluge
  A message of Peace they may bring.

    *   *   *   *   *   *

Do you ask me the place of the Valley,
  Ye hearts that are harrowed by Care?
It lieth afar between mountains,
  And God and His angels are there;
And one is the dark mount of Sorrow
  And one the bright mountain of Prayer.

GO, LOVELY ROSE.

BY EDMUND WALLER.

Edmund Waller was born in Hertfordshire, England, in 1605. He went to King's College, Cambridge. Later he entered parliament and took an active part in the long parliament. In 1664 he was exiled on account of participating in royalist plots. He returned to England under Cromwell's administration. He died at Beaconsfield in 1687. Waller's poems were first published in 1645

Go, lovely rose!
Tell her, that wastes her time and me,
  That now she knows,
When I resemble her to thee,
How sweet and fair she seems to be.

Tell her that's young
And shuns to have her graces spied
That hadst thou sprung
In deserts, where no men abide,
Thou must have uncommended died.

Small is the worth
Of beauty from the light retired;
Bid her come forth,
Suffer herself to be desired,
And not blush so to be admired.

Then die, that she
The common fate of all things rare
May read in thee;
How small a part of time they share
That are so wondrous sweet and fair!

THE LAST LEAF.

BY OLIVER WENDELL HOLMES

I saw him once before,
As he passed by the door,
    And again
The pavement stones resound,
As he totters o'er the ground
    With his cane.

They say that in his prime,
Ere the pruning-knife of Time
    Cut him down,
Not a better man was found
By the Crier on his round
    Through the town.

But now he walks the streets
And he looks at all he meets
    So forlorn;
And he shakes his feeble head,
That it seems as if he said,
    "They are gone."

The mossy marbles rest
On the lips that he has prest
    In their bloom,
And the names he loved to hear
Have been carved for many a year
    On the tomb.

*   *   *   *   *   *

And if I should live to be
The last leaf upon the tree
    In the spring,
Let them smile, as I do now,
At the old forsaken bough
    Where I cling.

THE SONG OF THE SHIRT.

BY THOMAS HOOD.

With fingers weary and worn,
　With eyelids heavy and red,
A woman sat in unwomanly rags,
　Plying her needle and thread—
Stitch! stitch! stitch!
　In poverty, hunger and dirt,
And still with a voice of dolorous pitch
　She sang the "Song of the Shirt!"

Work! work! work
　While the cock is crowing aloof!
And work—work—work,
　Till the stars shine through the roof!
It's oh! to be a slave
　Along with the barbarous Turk,
Where a woman has never a soul to save,
　If this is Christian work!

Work—work—work
　Till the brain begins to swim;
Work—work—work
　Till the eyes are heavy and dim!
Seam and gussett, and band,
　Band and gusset and seam,
Till over the buttons I fall asleep,
　And sew them on in a dream!

*　　*　　*　　*　　*　　*

Oh, men, with sisters dear!
　Oh, men, with mothers and wives!
It is not linen you're wearing out
　But human creature's lives!
Stitch—stitch—stitch,
　In poverty, hunger and dirt,
Sewing at once, with a double thread,
　A shroud as well as a shirt.

THE OLD OAKEN BUCKET.

BY SAMUEL WOODWORTH.

Samuel Woodworth was born at Scituate, Mass., in 1785, and was the son of a farmer and revolutionary soldier. He had no educational advantages until taken up by a clergyman, who had read some of his poetical writings and who gave him instruction in the classics. Woodworth was apprenticed to a printer, and later published a paper of his own, of which he was editor, printer, and carrier. Later he removed to New York, where he edited magazines and wrote a number of volumes. His patriotic songs of the war of 1812 were widely popular. His "Old Oaken Bucket" will always hold its place among the choicest songs of America. Woodworth died in New York in 1842.

How dear to this heart are the
    scenes of my childhood,
When fond recollection pre-
    sents them to view!
The orchard, the meadow, the
    deep-tangled wildwood,
And every loved spot which
    my infancy knew;
The wide-spreading pond, and
    the mill which stood by it
The bridge, and the rock
    where the cataract fell;
The cot of my father, the
    dairy-house nigh it,
And e'en the rude bucket
    which hung in the well—
The old oaken bucket, the
    iron-bound bucket,
The moss-covered bucket
    which hung in the well.

That moss-covered vessel I hail as a treasure;
    For often, at noon, when returned from the field,
I found it the source of an exquisite pleasure,
    The purest and sweetest that nature can yield.
How ardent I seized it, with hands that were glowing!
    And quick to the white-pebbled bottom it fell;

Then soon, with the emblem of truth overflowing,
   And dripping with coolness, it rose from the well—
The old oaken bucket, the iron-bound bucket,
The moss-covered bucket arose from the well.

How sweet from the green, mossy brim to receive it,
   As, poised on the curb, it inclined to my lips!
Not a full blushing goblet could tempt me to leave it,
   Though filled with the nectar that Jupiter sips.
And, now far removed from the loved situation,
   The tear of regret will intrusively swell,
As fancy reverts to my father's plantation,
   And sighs for the bucket which hangs in the well—
The old oaken bucket, the iron-bound bucket,
The moss-covered bucket which hangs in the well.

THE CHAMBERED NAUTILUS.
BY OLIVER WENDELL HOLMES.

This is the ship of pearl, which, poets feign,
   Sails the unshadowed main,—
   The venturesome bark that flings
On the sweet summer wind its purpled wings
In gulfs enchanted, where the Siren sings,
   And coral reefs lie bare,
Where the cold sea-maids rise to sun their streaming hair.

Its webs of living gauze no more unfurl;
   Wrecked is the ship of pearl!
   And every chambered cell,
Where its dim, dreaming life was wont to dwell,
As the frail tenant shaped his growing shell,
   Before thee lies revealed—
Its irised ceiling rent, its sunless crypt unsealed!

Year after year beheld the silent toil
   That spread his lustrous coil;
   Still, as the spiral grew,
He left the past year's dwelling for the new,
Stole with soft step its shining archway through,
   Built up its idle door,
Stretched in his last-found home, and knew the old no more.

87

Thanks for the heavenly message brought by thee,
    Child of the wandering sea,
    Cast from her lap, forlorn!
From thy dead lips a clearer note is born
Than ever Triton blew from wreathed horn!
    While on mine ear it rings,
Through the deep caves of thought I hear a voice that sings:—

Build thee more stately mansions, O, my soul,
    As the swift seasons roll!
    Leave thy low-vaulted past!
Let each new temple, nobler than the last,
Shut thee from heaven with a dome more vast,
    Till thou at length art free,
Leaving thine outgrown shell by life's unresting sea!

"ONE TOUCH OF NATURE."

WILLIAM SHAKSPEARE.

["From Troilus and Cressida."]

For time is like a fashionable
host
That slightly shakes his part-
ing guest by the hand,
And with his arms outstretched,
as he would fly,
Grasps—in the comer; welcome
ever smiles,
And farewell goes out sighing.
O, let not virtue seek
Remuneration for the thing it
was;
For beauty, wit,
High birth, vigor of bone, de-
sert in service,
Love, friendship, charity, are
subjects all

To envious and calumniating time.
One touch of nature makes the whole world
kin—
That all, with one consent, praise new-born
gauds,
Though they are made and molded of things
past,
And give to dust that is a little gilt
More laud than gilt o'er dusted.

A REQUIEM.

BY ROBERT LOUIS STEVENSON.

Robert Louis Stevenson, the son of a lighthouse engineer, was born at Edinburgh in 1850. He studied in the university of that city and became a lawyer, though he never practiced. On account of his ill-health he went to Samoa, where he lived with his family and wrote his books. He died in 1894. A few of his stories are: "Treasure Island," "Kidnapped," "New Arabian Nights," "St. Ives"; his essays are, "Virginibus Puerisque," "Travels of a Donkey in the Cevennes," and "Familiar Studies on Men and Books."

Under the wide and starry sky,
Dig the grave and let me lie,
Glad did I live and gladly die,
    And I laid me down with a will.

This be the verse you grave for me;
Here he lies where he longed to be;
Home is the sailor, home from the sea,
    And the hunter home from the hill.

REQUIESCAT

BY MATTHEW ARNOLD.

Matthew Arnold, son of the famous head master of Rugby, was born at Laleham, Middlesex, 1822. He studied at Winchester, Rugby, and Baliol college, Oxford, and was a fellow of Oriel. In 1851 he was made lay inspector of schools, and in '57 received the appointment of professor of poetry at Oxford. He died at Liverpool in 1888. He wrote "Empedocles on Etna," "Essays in Criticism," "Study of Celtic Literature," "Culture and Anarchy," and other books of essays.

    Strew on her roses, roses,
        And never a spray of yew!
    In quiet she reposes;
        Ah! would that I did, too.

Her mirth the world required;
   She bathed it in smiles of glee,
But her heart was tired, tired,
   And now they let her be.

Her life was turning, turning,
   In mazes of heat and sound;
But for peace her soul was yearning,
   And now peace laps her round.

Her cabin'd ample spirit,
   It flutter'd and fail'd for breath;
To-night it doth inherit
   The vasty hall of death.

AT THE CHURCH GATE.

BY W. M. THACKERAY.

William Makepeace Thackeray was born at Calcutta in 1811. He was brought up in England, where he went to Charterhouse school and later to Trinity college, Cambridge. He left college after one year's study and went to Paris, where he studied with the hope of becoming an artist. His first contributions in the way of writing were to Frazer's Magazine, and among them were his famous "Yellowplush Papers." He wrote other satires and humorous ballads for Punch. Thackeray was the first editor of the Cornhill Magazine, which is still in publication. He died in London in 1863.

Although I enter not,
Yet round about the spot
    Ofttimes I hover;
And near the sacred gate,
With longing eyes I wait,
    Expectant of her.

My lady comes at last,
Timid and stepping fast,
    And hastening hither
With modest eyes downcast;
She comes—she's here, she's past!
    May heaven go with her!

Kneel undisturbed, fair saint!
Pour out your praise or plaint
    Meekly and duly;
I will not enter there,
To sully your pure prayer
    With thoughts unruly.

But suffer me to pace
Round the forbidden place,
    Lingering a minute,
Like outcast spirits who wait,
And see, through heaven's gate,
    Angels within it.

HE'D HAD NO SHOW.

BY SAM WALTER FOSS.

Joe Beall 'ud set upon a keg
  Down to the groc'ry store, an' throw
One leg right over t'other leg
  An' swear he'd never had no show,
     "O, no," said Joe,
     "Hain't hed no show,"
Then shif his quid to t'other jaw,
An' chaw, an' chaw, an' chaw, an' chaw.

He said he got no start in life,
  Didn't get no money from his dad,
The washin' took in by his wife
  Earned all the funds he ever had.
     "O, no," said Joe,
     "Hain't hed no show,"
An' then he'd look up at the clock
An' talk, an' talk, an' talk, an' talk.

"I've waited twenty year—let's see—
  Yes, twenty-four, an' never struck,
Altho' I've sot roun' patiently,
  The fust tarnation streak er luck,

     O, no," said Joe,
     "Hain't hed no show,"
Then stuck like mucilage to the spot,
An' sot, an' sot, an' sot, an' sot.

"I've come down regerler every day
  For twenty years to Piper's store.
I've sot here in a patient way,
  Say, hain't I, Piper?" Piper swore.
     "I tell ye, Joe,
     Yer hain't no show;
Yer too dern patient"—ther hull raft
Jest laffed, an' laffed, an' laffed, an' laffed.

TO THE CUCKOO.

BY JOHN LOGAN.

John Logan was born in Scotland in 1748. He wrote lyric poems and
published his poems in collaboration with Michael Bruce in 1770. This
double volume of poems led probably to the confusion of the authorship
of the "Ode to the Cuckoo." The question is still debated, but the poem
is generally attributed to Logan. He died in 1788 at London.

Hail beauteous stranger of the
    grove!
  Thou messenger of Spring!
Now Heaven repairs thy rural
    seat,
  And woods thy welcome ring.

What time the daisy decks the
    green,
  Thy certain voice we hear;
Hast thou a star to guide thy path,
  Or mark the rolling year?

Delightful visitant! with thee
  I hail the time of flowers,
And hear the sound of music
    sweet
  From birds among the bowers.

*   *   *   *

Sweet bird! thy bower is ever green,
  Thy sky is ever clear;
Thou hast no sorrow in thy song,
  No winter in thy year!

O, could I fly, I'd fly with thee!
  We'd make, with joyful wing,
Our annual visit oe'r the globe,
  Companions of the Spring.

HER MORAL.

BY THOMAS HOOD.

Gold! Gold! Gold! Gold!
Bright and yellow, hard and cold,
Molten, graven, hammered, and rolled;
Heavy to get, and light to hold;
Hoarded, bartered, bought, and sold,
Stolen, borrowed, squandered, doled;
Spurned by the young, but hugged by
    the old
To the very verge of the churchyard
    mould;
Price of many a crime untold.

Gold! Gold! Gold! Gold!
Good or bad a thousandfold!
How widely its agencies vary—
To save—to ruin—to curse—to bless—
As even its minted coins express,
Now stamp'd with the image of Good
    Queen Bess
And now of a bloody Mary.

SERENADE.

BY HENRY W. LONGFELLOW.

Stars of the summer night!
  Far in yon azure deeps,
Hide, hide your golden light!
  She sleeps!
My lady sleeps!
  Sleeps!

Moon of the summer night!
  Far down yon western steeps,
Sink, sink in silver light!
  She sleeps!
My lady sleeps!
  Sleeps!

Wind of the summer night!
  Where yonder woodbine creeps,
Fold, fold thy pinions light!
  She sleeps!
My lady sleeps!
  Sleeps!

Dreams of the summer night!
  Tell her, her lover keeps
Watch, while in slumbers light
  She sleeps!
My lady sleeps!
  Sleeps!

ODE ON A GRECIAN URN.

BY JOHN KEATS.

John Keats was born at London in 1795. He studied medicine, but after passing his examinations he never practiced. About this time he became acquainted with Shelley, Leigh Hunt, and Haydon. In 1820 he went to Naples on account of his health, and from there to Rome, where he died in 1821. His longer poems are: "Endymion" (which poem was most severely criticised at the time of its publication), "Lamia," "Isabella," and "The Eve of Saint Agnes."

Thou still unravished bride of
    quietness,
  Thou foster child of Silence
    and slow Time,
Sylvan historian, who canst thus
    express
  A flowery tale more sweetly
    than our rhyme;
What leaf-fring'd legend haunts
    about thy shape
  Of deities or mortals, or of
    both,
In Tempe or the dales of Arcady?
  What men or gods are these?
    What maidens loath?
What mad pursuit? What strug-
    gles to escape?
  What pipes and timbrels?
    What wild ecstasy?

Heard melodies are sweet, but
    those unheard
  Are sweeter; therefore, ye soft
    pipes, play on;
Not to the sensual ear, but, more
    endeared,
  Pipe to the spirit ditties of no
    tone;

Fair youth, beneath the trees, thou canst not leave
  Thy song, nor ever can those trees be bare;
Bold lover, never, never canst thou kiss,
  Though winning near the goal—yet do not grieve,
She cannot fade, though thou hast not thy bliss,
  For ever wilt thou love, and she be fair!

O, Attic shape! Fair attitude! with brede
  Of marble men and maidens overwrought,
With forest branches and the trodden weed;
  Thou, silent form, dost tease us out of thought
As doth eternity: Cold pastoral!
  When old age shall this generation waste,
Thou shalt remain, in midst of other woe
  Than ours, a friend to man to whom thou say'st,
"Beauty is truth, truth beauty"—that is all
  Ye know on earth, truth, and all ye need to know.

TO ALTHEA FROM PRISON.

BY RICHARD LOVELACE.

This lyric of Richard Lovelace's is, with the "Lucasta," the best known and most often quoted of his poems.

When Love with unconfined wings
  Hovers within my gates,
And my divine Althea brings
  To whisper at my grates;
When I lie tangled in her hair
  And fettered with her eye,
The birds that wanton in the air
  Know no such liberty

When flowing cups pass swiftly round
  With no allaying Thames,
Our careless heads with roses crowned,
  Our hearts with loyal flames;
When thirsty grief in wine we steep,
  When healths and draughts go free—
Fishes that tipple in the deep
  Know no such liberty.

When linnet-like confined,
  With shriller throat shall sing
Thy mercy, sweetness, majesty
  And glories of my king;
When I shall voice aloud how good
  He is, how great should be,
The enlarged winds that curl the flood
  Know no such liberty.

Stone walls do not a prison make,
  Nor iron bars a cage;
Minds innocent and quiet take
  That for a hermitage;
If I have freedom in my love
  And in my soul am free,
Angels alone, that soar above,
  Enjoy such liberty.

99

SONG.

BY JOHN BUNYAN.

John Bunyan was born at Elstow in 1628. He was a tinker, as his father was before him, but he finally became a soldier in the parliamentary army. In 1653 he became a nonconformist and went about the country preaching until he was arrested under the statutes against that doctrine. While in prison Bunyan began his well-known allegory—"Pilgrim's Progress." Under Charles II. he was released and made pastor at Bedford. He died at London in 1688.

He that is down need fear no fall;
　He that is low, no pride;
He that is humble ever shall
　Have God to be his guide.

I am content with what I have,
　Little be it or much;
And, Lord, contentment still I crave,
　Because thou savest such.

Fullness to such a burden is
　That go on pilgrimage;
Here little, and hereafter bliss,
　Is best from age to age.

BELIEVE ME, IF ALL THOSE ENDEARING YOUNG CHARMS.

BY THOMAS MOORE.

In the early part of the last century when the star of Moore was at its zenith, no song was more popular than this, perhaps as much for the charming air to which it is set as for the beauty and rhythm of its words.

Believe me, if all those endearing charms,
    Which I gaze on so fondly today,
Were to change by tomorrow, and fleet in my arms,
    Like fairy-gifts fading away,
Thou wouldst still be ador'd, as this moment thou art,
    Let thy loveliness fade as it will
And around the dear ruin each wish of my heart
    Would entwine itself verdantly still.

It is not while beauty and youth are thine own,
    And thy cheeks unprofan'd by a tear,
That the fervor and faith of a soul can be known,
    To which time will but make thee more dear;
No, the heart that has truly loved never forgets,
    But as surely loves on to the close,
As the sunflower turns on her god, when he sets,
    The same look that she turned when he rose.

THE WORLD IS TOO MUCH WITH US.

BY WILLIAM WORDSWORTH.

The world is too much with us; late
    and soon,
Getting and spending, we lay waste
    our powers;
Little we see in nature that is ours;
We have given our hearts away, a
    sordid boon!
This sea that bares her bosom to
    the moon;
The winds that will be howling at all hours,
And are up-gathered now like sleeping flowers;
For this, for everything, we are out of tune;
It moves us not—Great God! I'd rather be
A Pagan suckled in a creed outworn,
So might I, standing on this pleasant lea,
Have glimpses that would make me less for-
    lorn;
Have sight of Proteus rising from the sea,
Or hear old Triton blow his wreathed horn!

ODE ON SOLITUDE

BY ALEXANDER POPE.

Pope was born at London in 1688. He had no school education, as he
was always sickly, but he learned Latin and Greek from several friends.
By the time he was 17 he was an acknowledged wit and critic. His first
published poem was "The Pastorals," 1709; then followed "The Rape of
the Lock," his best satirical poem, and the next year (1713) he began his
translation of the "Iliad." He died at Twickenham in 1744.

Happy the man whose wish and care
  A few paternal acres bound,
Content to breathe his native air
  In his own ground.

Whose herds with milk, whose fields with bread,
  Whose flocks supply him with attire;
Whose trees in summer yield him shade,
  In winter fire.

Blest, who can unconcern'dly find
  Hours, days, and years slide soft away;
In health of body, peace of mind,
  Quiet by day,

Sound sleep by night, study and ease,
  Together mixt, sweet recreation;
And innocence, which most doth please,
  With meditation.

Thus let me live, unseen, unknown;
  Thus, unlamented, let me die,
Steal from the world, and not a stone
  Tell where I lie.

PATRIOTISM.

BY SIR WALTER SCOTT.

Sir Walter Scott was born at Edinburgh in 1771. He first began his writing by translating Burger and Goethe, but he left this work to take up the Border Minstrelsy of his own country. In 1814 he published the first of the well-known "Waverley" novels. He sold his copyrights to the firm of Constable, and as the house failed a few years later Scott was heavily involved. As he had also recently bought and repaired the estate of Abbotsford, he was in debt for that also. In spite of ill health he wrote incessantly in order to meet his bills, and gave to the world the novels and poems with which all are so familiar. He died in 1832.

Unwept. Unhonored and Unsung.

Breathes there a man with soul so dead
Who never to himself hath said,
"This is my own, my native land!"
Whose heart hath ne'er within him burned
As home his footsteps he hath turned
From wandering on a foreign strand?
If such there breathe, go, mark him well!
For him no minstrel raptures swell;
High though his titles, proud his name,
Boundless his wealth as wish can claim—
Despite those titles, power, and pelf,
The wretch, concentered all in self,
Living, shall forfeit fair renown,
And, doubly dying, shall go down
To the vile dust from whence he sprung,
Unwept, unhonored, and unsung.

ROCKED IN THE CRADLE OF THE DEEP.

BY EMMA WILLARD.

Emma Willard, the American educator and author, was one of a family of seventeen children. Her maiden name was Hart. She was born at Berlin, Conn., in 1787. She began teaching in the village school and later became principal of a girls' college at Westfield, Conn., and after her marriage to Dr. John Willard in 1814, opened a boarding school at Middlebury, Conn., into which she introduced new methods and new studies. The school was removed to Troy, N. Y., and became the Troy Female Academy. Retiring from the school in 1858, Mrs. Willard spent the remaining years of her life in revising her text books and writing a volume of poems. She died in 1876.

Rocked in the cradle of the deep.
I lay me down in peace to sleep;
Secure I rest upon the wave,
For Thou, O Lord, hast power to save.

I know Thou wilt not slight my call,
For Thou dost mark the sparrow's fall;
And calm and peaceful is my sleep,
Rocked in the cradle of the deep.

And such the trust that still were mine,
Though stormy winds swept o'er the brine,
Or though the tempest's fiery breath
Roused me from sleep to wreck and death.

In ocean's caves still safe with Thee,
The germ of immortality;
And calm and peaceful is my sleep,
Rocked in the cradle of the deep.

THE CRY OF THE CHILDREN.

BY ELIZABETH BARRETT BROWNING.

The influence of poetry is greater than is generally realized, and many find inspiration to action in reading it. Mrs. Browning in this pathetic poem did much to rouse England to the evil of child labor and to perceive the wrongs done the little ones toiling in its factories and coal mines far beyond their strength.

Do ye hear the children weeping, O, my brothers,
    Ere the sorrow comes with years?
They are leaning their young heads against their mothers,
    And that cannot stop their tears.

But the young, young children, O, my brothers,
    They are weeping bitterly!
They are weeping in the playtime of the others,
    In the country of the free.

Still, all day, the iron wheels go onward,
    Grinding life down from its mark;
And the children's souls which God is calling sunward,
    Spin on blindly in the dark.

ABOU BEN ADHEM AND THE ANGEL.

BY LEIGH HUNT.

James Henry Leigh Hunt was born at Southgate in 1784. He was an essayist, an author, and a poet, chief among his poems being "The Story of Rimini." He died at Putney in 1859.

Abou Ben Adhem (may his tribe increase!)
Awoke one night from a deep dream of peace,
And saw, within the moonlight of his room,
Making it rich, and like a lily in bloom,
An angel writing in a book of gold—
Exceeding peace had made Ben Adhem bold,
And to the presence in the room he said,
"What writest thou?" The vision raised its head,
And with a look made all of sweet accord,
Answer'd, "The names of those who love the Lord."
"And is mine one?" said Abou. "Nay, not so,"
Replied the angel. Abou spoke more low,
But cheerily still, and said, "I pray thee, then,
Write me as one who loves his fellowmen."
The angel wrote and vanish'd. The next night
It came again with a great wakening light,
And show'd the names whom love of God had bless'd,
And lo! Ben Adhem's name led all the rest.

BUGLE SONG.

BY ALFRED TENNYSON.

This poem is one of the lyrics from the "Princess," yet there is so little connection between the story and these five or six charming songs embedded within the mock heroic poem that one does not think of them as part of the medley.

The splendor falls on castle walls
   And snowy summits old in story:
The long light shakes across the lakes,
   And the wild cataract leaps in glory.
Blow, bugle, blow, set the wild echoes flying,
Blow, bugle; answer, echoes, dying, dying, dying.

O hark, O hear! how thin and clear,
   And thinner, clearer, farther going!
O sweet and far from cliff and scar
The horns of Elfland faintly blowing!
Blow, let us hear the purple glens replying;
Blow, bugle; answer, echoes, dying, dying, dying.

O love, they die in yon rich sky,
   They faint on hill or field or river:
Our echoes roll from soul to soul,
   And grow forever and forever.
Blow, bugle, blow, set the wild echoes flying,
And answer echoes, answer, dying, dying, dying.

OPPORTUNITY.

BY JOHN J. INGALLS.

John James Ingalls was born in Massachusetts in 1833 and was graduated from Williams College in 1855. He was admitted to the bar in 1857, and removed to Atchison, Kas., in 1859. He took an active interest in the exciting Kansas politics, and, besides serving as a delegate to the Wyandotte convention that framed the State constitution, he served as secretary to the Territorial Council. In 1862 he was a State Senator. He edited the Atchison Champion for three years and served in the State militia. In 1873 he was elected to the United States Senate, and then began his remarkably brilliant political career. After serving twenty years he was retired by the political revolution in his State. As an orator he held high rank. He frequently contributed to the leading magazines and reviews. He died about two years ago.

Master of human destinies am I.
Fame, love, and fortune on my footsteps
    wait,
Cities and fields I walk; I penetrate
Deserts and seas remote, and, passing by
Hovel, and mart, and palace, soon or late
I knock unbidden once at every gate!
If sleeping, wake—if feasting, rise before
I turn away.   It is the hour of fate,
And they who follow me reach every state
Mortals desire, and conquer every foe
Save death; but those who doubt or
    hesitate,
Condemned to failure, penury and woe,
Seek me in vain and uselessly implore—
I answer not, and I return no more.

MIGNON'S SONG FROM "WILHELM MEISTER."

"After having sung the song a second time, she paused for a moment, and, attentively surveying Wilhelm, she asked him, 'Know'st thou the land?' 'It must be Italy!' he replied."—Wilhelm Meister's Apprenticeship.

Know'st thou the land where the lemon tree blows—
Where deep in the bower the gold orange grows?
Where zephyrs from heaven die softly away,
And the laurel and myrtle tree never decay?
Know'st thou it?   Thither, O! thither with thee,
My dearest, my fondest! with thee would I flee.

Know'st thou the hall with its pillared arcades,
Its chambers so vast and its long colonnades?
Where the statues of marble with features so mild
Ask "Why have they used thee so harshly, my child?"
Know'st thou it?   Thither, O! thither with thee,
My guide, my protector! with thee would I flee.

Know'st thou the Alp which the vapor enshrouds,
Where the bold muleteer seeks his way thro' the clouds?
In the cleft of the mountain the dragon abides,
And the rush of the stream tears the rock from its sides;
Know'st thou it?   Thither, O! thither with thee,
Leads our way, father—then come, let us flee.

PSALM LXXXIV.

How amiable are thy tabernacles, O Lord of hosts!

My soul longeth, yea, even fainteth for the courts of the Lord; my heart and my flesh crieth out for the living God.

Yea, the sparrow hath found an house, and the swallow a nest for herself, where she may lay her young, even thine altars, O Lord of hosts, my King and my God.

Blessed are they that dwell in thy house; they will be still praising thee. Selah.

Blessed is the man whose strength is in thee; in whose heart are the ways of them.

Who, passing through the valley of Baca, make it a well; the rain also filleth the pools.

They go from strength to strength; every one of them in Zion appeareth before God.

O Lord God of hosts, hear my prayer; give ear, O God of Jacob. Selah.

Behold, O God our shield, and look upon the face of thine anointed.

For a day in thy courts is better than a thousand. I had rather be a doorkeeper in the house of my God than to dwell in the tents of wickedness.

For the Lord God is a sun and shield; the Lord will give grace and glory; no good thing will he withhold from them that walk uprightly.

O Lord of hosts, blessed is the man that trusteth in thee.

THANATOPSIS.

BY WILLIAM CULLEN BRYANT.

This imperishable poem was written by William Cullen Bryant when he was 18 years old. It was sent to the North American Review either by the poet or his father. Richard Henry Dana of the Review supposed the writer to be some one of international repute. The poet's father was then a member of the Massachusetts senate. Dana went to the statehouse to call on him, but the appearance of Dr. Bryant seemed to satisfy Dana that he must look elsewhere for the author, and so he returned to Cambridge without an interview with the senator. Later he learned that the author was the doctor's son.

To him who, in the love of nature, holds
Communion with her visible forms, she speaks
A various language; for his gayer hours
She has a voice of gladness and a smile
And eloquence of beauty; and she glides
Into his darker musings with a mild
And healing sympathy, that steals away
Their sharpness, ere he is aware. When thoughts
Of the last bitter hour come like a blight
Over thy spirit, and sad images
Of the stern agony, and shroud, and pall,
And breathless darkness, and the narrow house,
Make thee to shudder and grow sick at heart,
Go forth under the open sky, and list
To Nature's teachings, while from all around—
Earth and her waters, and the depths of air—
Comes a still voice: Yet a few days, and thee
The all-beholding sun shall see no more
In all his course; nor yet in the cold ground

Where thy pale form was laid, with many tears,
Nor in the embrace of ocean, shall exist
Thy image. Earth, that nourished thee, shall claim
Thy growth, to be resolved to earth again;
And, lost each human trace, surrendering up
Thine individual being, shalt thou go
To mix forever with the elements;
To be a brother to the insensible rock,
And to the sluggish clod, which the rude swain
Turns with his share, and treads upon. The oak
Shall send his roots abroad, and pierce thy mold.
Yet not to thine eternal resting place
Shalt thou retire alone—nor couldst thou wish
Couch more magnificent. Thou shalt lie down
With patriarchs of the infant world—with kings,
The powerful of the earth—the wise, the good,
Fair forms, and hoary seers of ages past,
All in one mighty sepulcher. The hills,
Rock-ribbed, and ancient as the sun; the vales
Stretching in pensive quietness between;
The venerable woods; rivers that move
In majesty, and the complaining brooks,
That make the meadows green; and, poured round all,
Old ocean's gray and melancholy waste—
Are but the solemn decorations all
Of the great tomb of man! The golden sun,
The planets, all the infinite host of heaven,
Are shining on the sad abodes of death,
Through the still lapse of ages. All that tread
The globe are but a handful to the tribes
That slumber in its bosom. Take the wings
Of morning, pierce the Barcan wilderness,
Or lose thyself in the continuous woods
Where rolls the Oregon and hears no sound
Save his own dashings—yet the dead are there!
And millions in those solitudes, since first
The flight of years began, have laid them down
In their last sleep—the dead reign there alone!
So shalt thou rest; and what if thou withdraw

In silence from the living, and no friend
Take note of thy departure? All that breathe
Will share thy destiny. The gay will laugh
When thou art gone, the solemn brood of care
Plod on, and each one, as before, will chase
His favorite phantom; yet all these shall leave
Their mirth and their employments, and shall come
And make their bed with thee. As the long train
Of ages glides away, the sons of men—
The youth in life's green spring, and he who goes
In the full strength of years, matron and maid,
And the sweet babe, and the gray headed man—
Shall, one by one, be gathered to thy side
By those who in their turn shall follow them.

So live, that when thy summons comes to join
The innumerable caravan that moves
To the pale realms of shade, where each shall take
His chamber in the silent halls of death,
Thou go not, like the quarry slave at night,
Scourged to his dungeon, but, sustained and soothed
By an unfaltering trust, approach thy grave
Like one who wraps the drapery of his couch
About him, and lies down to pleasant dreams.

THE NIGHT HAS A THOUSAND EYES.

BY FRANCIS WILLIAM BOURDILLON.

Francis William Bourdillon was born in Woolbedding in 1852. He received his education at Worcester College, Oxford, and was afterwards a private tutor to the sons of the Prince and Princess Christian. A few of his published works are, "Among the Flowers and Other Poems," 1874; "Ailes d'Alouette," 1891; "A Lost God," 1892; and "Sursum Corda," 1893.

THE night has a thousand eyes,
    And the day but one;
Yet the light of the bright world dies
    With the dying sun.

THE mind has a thousand eyes,
    And the heart but one;
Yet the light of a whole life dies
    When love is done.

THE HERITAGE.

BY JAMES RUSSELL LOWELL.

The rich man's son inherits lands,
  And piles of brick, and stone, and gold,
And he inherits soft, white hands,
  And tender flesh that fears the cold,
  Nor dares to wear a garment old;
A heritage, it seems to me,
One scarce would wish to hold in fee.

The rich man's son inherits cares;
  The bank may break, the factory burn,
A breath may burst his bubble shares;
  And soft, white hands could scarcely earn
  A living that would serve his turn;
A heritage, it seems to me,
One scarce would wish to hold in fee.

The rich man's son inherits wants,
  His stomach craves for dainty fare;
With sated heart he hears the pants
  Of toiling hinds with brown arms bare,
  And wearies in his easy chair;
A heritage, it seems to me,
One scarce would wish to hold in fee.

What doth the poor man's son inherit?
  Stout muscles and a sinewy heart,
A hardy frame, a hardier spirit;
  King of two hands, he does his part
  In every useful toil and art;
A heritage, it seems to me,
A king might wish to hold in fee.

What doth the poor man's son inherit?
  Wishes o'erjoyed with humble things,
A rank adjudged by toil-worn merit,
  Content that from employment springs.
  A heart that in his labor sings;
A heritage, it seems to me,
A king might wish to hold in fee.

What doth the poor man's son inherit?
  A patience learned of being poor;
Courage, if sorrow come, to bear it.
  A fellow-feeling that is sure
  To make the outcast bless his door;
A heritage, it seems to me,
A king might wish to hold in fee.

O, rich man's son! there is a toil
  That with all others level stands;
Large charity doth never soil,
  But only whiten, soft white hands—
  This is the best crop from thy lands;
A heritage, it seems to me,
Worth being rich to hold in fee.

O, poor man's son! scorn not thy state;
  There is worse weariness than thine,
In merely being rich and great;
  Toil only gives the soul to shine,
  And makes rest fragrant and benign—
A heritage, it seems to me,
Worth being poor to hold in fee.

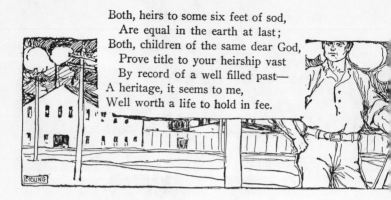

Both, heirs to some six feet of sod,
   Are equal in the earth at last;
Both, children of the same dear God,
   Prove title to your heirship vast
   By record of a well filled past—
A heritage, it seems to me,
Well worth a life to hold in fee.

A DITTY.

BY SIR PHILIP SIDNEY.

My true love hath my heart, and I have his,
   By just exchange one to the other given;
I hold his dear, and mine he cannot miss,
   There never was a better bargain driven;
My true love hath my heart and I have his.

His heart in me keeps him and me in one,
   My heart in him his thoughts and senses guides;
He loves my heart, for once it was his own,
   I cherish his because in me it bides:
My true love hath my heart and I have his.

PSALM CXXI.

I will lift up mine eyes unto the hills, from whence cometh my help.

My help cometh from the Lord, which made heaven and earth.

He will not suffer thy foot to be moved; he that keepeth thee will not slumber.

Behold, he that keepeth Israel shall neither slumber nor sleep.

The Lord is thy keeper; the Lord is thy shade upon thy right hand.

The sun shall not smite thee by day, nor the moon by night.

The Lord shall preserve thee from all evil; he shall preserve thy soul.

The Lord shall preserve thy going out and thy coming in from this time forth and even for evermore.

THE STAR SPANGLED BANNER.

BY FRANCIS SCOTT KEY.

Francis Scott Key was born in Frederick County, Maryland, in 1780. He was the author of a volume of poems published in 1857, but the poem that will keep him alive in the memory of the nation is his "Star Spangled Banner." This poem was written on shipboard during the war of 1812, while the English were bombarding Fort McHenry. Mr. Key died at Baltimore in 1843.

O! say, can you see, by the dawn's early light,
    What so proudly we hailed at the twilight's last gleaming?
Whose broad stripes and bright stars thro' the perilous fight,
    O'er the ramparts we watched were so gallantly streaming!
And the rocket's red glare, the bombs bursting in air,
Gave proof thro' the night that our flag was still there;
O! say, does that star spangled banner yet wave
O'er the land of the free and the home of the brave?

On that shore, dimly seen thro' the mists of the deep,
    Where the foe's haughty host in dread silence reposes,
What is that which the breeze, o'er the towering steep,
    As it fitfully blows, now conceals, now discloses?
Now it catches the gleam of the morning's first beam,
In full glory reflected, now shines on the stream;
'Tis the star spangled banner, O, long may it wave
O'er the land of the free and the home of the brave!

And where is that band who so vauntingly swore
    That the havoc of war and the battle's confusion,
A home and a country should leave us no more?
    Their blood has washed out their foul footsteps' pollution;
No refuge could save the hireling and slave
From the terror of flight or the gloom of the grave.
And the star spangled banner in triumph doth wave
O'er the land of the free and the home of the brave!

O! thus be it ever when freemen shall stand
  Between their loved homes and the war's desolation;
Blest with vict'ry and peace, may the heav'n-rescued land
  Praise the Power that hath made and preserved us a nation.
Then conquer we must when our cause it is just,
And this be our motto, "In God is our trust."
And the star spangled banner in triumph shall wave
O'er the land of the free and the home of the brave!

FROM "IN MEMORIAM."

BY ALFRED TENNYSON.

O, yet we trust that somehow good
  Will be the final goal of ill,
  To pangs of nature, sins of will,
Defects of doubt, and taints of blood;

That nothing walks with aimless feet;
  That not one life shall be destroyed,
  Or cast as rubbish to the void,
When God hath made the pile complete;

That not a worm is cloven in vain,
  That not a moth with vain desire
  Is shriveled in a fruitless fire,
Or but subserves another's gain.

*   *   *   *   *   *   *

So runs my dream: But what am I?
  An infant crying in the night;
  An infant crying for the light;
And with no language but a cry.

The wish that of the living whole
  No life may fail beyond the grave,
  Derives it not from what we have
The likest God within the soul?

Are God and Nature then at strife,
  That Nature lends such evil dreams
  So careful of the type she seems,
So careless of the single life;

That I, considering everywhere
  Her secret meaning in her deeds,
  And finding that of fifty seeds
She often brings but one to bear

I falter where I firmly trod,
  And falling with my weight of cares
  Upon the great world's altar-stairs
That slope thro' darkness up to God

I stretch lame hands of faith, and grope,
  And gather dust and chaff, and call
  To what I feel is Lord of all,
And faintly trust the larger hope.

I REMEMBER, I REMEMBER.

BY THOMAS HOOD.

I remember, I remember
  The house where I was born,
The little window where the sun
  Came peeping in at morn;
He never came a wink too soon
  Nor brought too long a day;
But now, I often wish the night
  Had borne my breath away.

I remember, I remember
  Where I was used to swing,
And thought the air must rush as fresh
  To swallows on the wing;

My spirit flew in feathers then
  That is so heavy now,
And summer pools could hardly cool
  The fever on my brow.

I remember, I remember
  The fir trees dark and high;
I used to think their slender tops
  Were close against the sky;
It was a childish ignorance,
  But now 'tis little joy
To know I'm farther off from heaven
  Than when I was a boy.

MARY'S DREAM.

BY JOHN LOWE.

John Lowe, the author of this poem, was born at Kenmure, parish of Kells, Kircudbrightshire, Scotland, in 1750. His father was a gardener, and at the age of 14 John was apprenticed to a weaver, but in 1771 he was enabled to go to the University of Edinburg. Later he entered the family of Mr. McGhie or Airds, whose house was located on an elevated piece of ground washed by the Dee and Ken, a spot reverenced by Lowe for its beauty. Within the grounds he erected a rural seat environed with honeysuckle, woodbine, and other shrubs, which is known to this day as "Lowe's Seat," and there he composed many of his most beautiful verses.

The moon had climbed the highest hill
  That rises o'er the source of Dee,
And from the eastern summit shed
  Her silver light on tower and tree;
When Mary laid her down to sleep,
  Her thoughts on Sandy far at sea;
When, soft and low, a voice was heard,
  Saying, "Mary, weep no more for me."

She from her pillow gently raised
  Her head to ask who there might be,
And saw young Sandy shivering stand,
  With visage pale and hollow e'e.
"O, Mary dear, cold is my clay,
  It lies beneath a stormy sea;
Far, far from thee I sleep in death,
  So, Mary, weep no more for me.

"Three stormy nights and stormy days
   We tossed upon the raging main;
And long we strove our barque to save,
   But all our striving was in vain.
Even then, when horror chilled my blood,
   My heart was filled with love for thee.
The storm is past and I at rest,
   So, Mary, weep no more for me.

"O, maiden dear, thyself prepare!
   We soon shall meet upon that shore
Where love is free from doubt and care,
   And thou and I shall part no more!"
Loud crowed the cock, the shadow fled;
   No more of Sandy could she see,
But soft the passing spirit said,
   "Sweet Mary, weep no more for me!"

ON A BUST OF DANTE.

BY T. W. PARSONS.

Thomas William Parsons was born at Boston in 1818. He spent the greater part of his life in Europe. In 1867 he translated Dante's "Inferno." In 1854 he published, under the title "Ghetto di Roma," a collection of his poems. He died at Scituate, Mass., in 1892.

See, from his counterfeit of him
　Whom Arno shall remember long,
How stern of lineament, how grim,
　The father was of Tuscan song!
There but the burning sense of wrong,
　Perpetual care and scorn abide;
Small friendship for the lordly throng;
　Distrust of all the world beside.

126

Faithful if this wan image be,
    No dream his life was, but a fight;
Could any Beatrice see
    A lover in that anchorite?
To that cold Ghibeline's gloomy sight
    Who could have guessed the visions came
Of beauty, veiled with heavenly light,
    In circles of eternal flame?

The lips as Cumæ's cavern close,
    The cheeks with fast and sorrow thin,
The rigid front, almost morose,
    But for the patient hope within,
Declare a life whose course hath been
    Unsullied still, though still severe;
Which, through the wavering days of sin,
    Kept itself icy-chaste and clear.

Peace dwells not here—this rugged face
    Betrays no spirit of repose;
The sullen warrior sole we trace,
    The marble man of many woes.
Such was his mien when first arose
    The thought of that strange tale divine,
When hell he peopled with his foes,
    The scourge of many a guilty line.

BALLAD OF OLD TIME LADIES.

BY FRANCOIS VILLON.

This ballad, of which we give Dante Gabriel Rossetti's translation, was written by Villon in 1450. There are many translations of the poems of that beggar, poet, thief—that first lucid poet of France. Andrew Lang has interpreted him in one way, John Payne in another. The following translation is, perhaps, the happiest of this particular poem, though the ballad cannot but lose some of its spirit in an English rendering.

Tell me, now, in what hidden way is
    Lady Flora the lovely Roman?
Where's Hipparchia, and where is Thais—
    Neither of them the fairer woman?
Where is Echo, beheld of no man,
    Only heard on river and mere—
She whose beauty was more than human?
    But where are the snows of yesteryear?

Where's Heloise, the learned nun,
    For whose sake Abeillard, I ween,
Lost manhood and put priesthood on?
    (From love he won such dule and teen!)
And where, I pray you, is the Queen
    Who willed that Buridan should steer,
Sewed in a sack's mouth, down the Seine?
    But where are the snows of yesteryear?

White Queen Blanche, like a queen of lilies
    With a voice like any mermaiden—
Bertha Broadfoot, Beatrice, Alice,
    And Ermengarde, the lady of the Maine—
And that good Joan, whom Englishmen
    At Rouen doomed, and burned her there
Mother of God, where are they, then?
    But where are the snows of yesteryear?

Nay, never ask this week, fair lord,
    Where they are gone, nor yet this year,
Except with this for an overword—
    But where are the snows of yesteryear?

SONG OF THE WESTERN MEN.

BY ROBERT STEPHEN HAWKER.

Mr. Hawker was a clergyman, born at Plymouth, England, in 1804, and died there in 1875. He was educated at Oxford and became a noted figure in the church. He was a stalwart and heroic character. In 1834 he became vicar of a lonely parish on the Cornwall coast. His "Echoes From Old Cornwall" appeared in 1845; "Cornish Ballads" in 1869. Shortly before his death he joined the Roman Catholic Church.

A good sword and a trusty hand!
  And merry heart and true!
King James' men shall understand
  What Cornish lads can do.

And have they fixed the where and when?
  And shall Trelawney die?
Here's twenty thousand Cornish men
  Will know the reason why!

Out spake their Captain brave and bold,
  A merry wight was he;
"If London Tower were Michael's hold,
  We'll set Trelawney free!

"We'll cross the Tamar, land to land,
  The Severn is no stay;
With 'one and all' and hand in hand,
  And who shall bid us nay?

"And when we come to London Wall,
  A pleasant sight to view,
Come forth! Come forth, ye cowards all,
  Here's men as good as you!

"Trelawney he's in keep and hold,
  Trelawney he may die;
But here's twenty thousand Cornish bold,
  Will know the reason why!"

THE SHEPHERDESS.

BY ALICE MEYNELL.

Mrs. Meynell is considered by many critics as the most elegant poet in England at this present time. She has written, besides several volumes of verse, two or three books of essays: "The Color of Life," "The Rhythm of Life," and "The Children."

She walks—the lady of my delight—
    A shepherdess of sheep.
Her flocks are thoughts. She keeps them white;
    She guards them from the steep.
She feeds them on the fragrant height,
    And folds them in for sleep.

She roams maternal hills and bright,
    Dark valleys safe and deep.
Into her tender breast at night
    The chastest stars may peep.
She walks—the lady of my delight—
    A shepherdess of sheep.

She holds her little thoughts in sight,
  Though gay they run and leap.
She is so circumspect and right;
  She has her soul to keep.
She walks—the lady of my delight—
  A shepherdess of sheep.

INVICTUS.

BY W. E. HENLEY.

William Ernest Henley was born in England about 1850. In 1888 he became editor of the Scots Observer, and in the same year published his first volume of poems—"A Book of Verses." He is a writer and a critic as well as a poet.

Out of the night that covers me,
  Black as the pit from pole to pole,
I thank whatever gods may be
  For my unconquerable soul.

In the fell clutch of circumstance
  I have not winced nor cried aloud;
Under the bludgeonings of chance
  My head is bloody, but unbow'd.

Beyond this place of wrath and tears
  Looms but the Horror of the shade,
And yet the menace of the years
  Finds and shall find me unafraid.

It matters not how straight the gate,
  How charged with punishments the scroll,
I am the master of my fate;
  I am the captain of my soul.

'TIS THE LAST ROSE OF SUMMER.

BY THOMAS MOORE.

'Tis the last rose of summer
　Left blooming alone;
All her lovely companions
　Are faded and gone;
No flower of her kindred,
　No rosebud is nigh,
To reflect back her blushes,
　Or give sigh for sigh,

I'll not leave thee, thou lone one!
　To pine on the stem;
Since the lovely are sleeping,
　Go, sleep thou with them.

Thus kindly I scatter
  Thy leaves o'er the bed,
Where thy mates of the garden
  Lie scentless and dead.

So soon may I follow,
  When friendships decay,
And from love's shining circle
  The gems drop away!
When true hearts lie withered,
  And fond ones are flown,
Oh, who would inhabit
  This bleak world alone?

MUSIC, WHEN SOFT VOICES DIE.
BY PERCY BYSSHE SHELLEY.

Music, when soft voices die,
Vibrates in the memory;
Odors, when sweet violets sicken,
Live within the sense they quicken.

Rose leaves, when the rose is dead,
Are heapt for the belovèd bed;
And so thy thoughts when thou art gone,
Love itself shall slumber on.

A SEA SONG.

BY ALLAN CUNNINGHAM.

"And who shall sing the glory of the deep" better than Allan Cunningham has done in this song of a sailor's love, a poet's love, for the sea?

A wet sheet and a flowing sea,
    And a wind that follows fast,
And fills the white and rustling sail,
    And bends the gallant mast;
And bends the gallant mast, my boys,
    While, like the eagle free,
Away the good ship flies, and leaves
    Old England on the lee.

Oh, for a soft and gentle wind!
    I heard a fair one cry;
But give to me the snoring breeze
    And white waves heaving high;

And white waves heaving high, my boys,
    The good ship tight and free;
The world of waters is our home,
    And merry men are we.
There's tempest in yon horned moon,
    And lightning in yon cloud;
And hark the music, mariners!
    The wind is piping loud;
The wind is piping loud, my boys,
    The lightning flashing free—
While the hollow oak our palace is,
    Our heritage the sea.

SONG FROM "PIPPA PASSES."

BY ROBERT BROWNING.

Robert Browning was born at Camberwell in 1812. He was educated
at the London University. While his wife lived Browning spent most
of his time in Florence—later he divided his time between London and
Venice. He died at Venice in 1889. His poems have been collected into
several volumes under the titles of "Men and Women," "Dramatis Per-
sonae," "The Ring and the Book," "Dramatic Idylls," and "Sordello."

The year's at the spring,
And day's at the morn;
Morning's at seven;
The hillside's dew-pearled.
The lark's on the wing;
The snail's on the thorn;
God's in his heaven—
All's right with the world!

THE WAITING.

BY JOHN G. WHITTIER.

John Greenleaf Whittier was born in Massachusetts in 1807. He was successively the editor of the "American Manufacturer," the "Haverhill Gazette," and the "New England Weekly Review." In 1836 he went to Philadelphia to edit the "Pennsylvania Freeman," for he was an abolitionist of strong principle. He died in 1892.

I wait and watch; before my eyes
    Methinks the night grows thin and gray;
I wait and watch the eastern skies
To see the golden spears uprise
    Beneath the oriflamme of day!

Like one whose limbs are bound in trance
    I hear the day-sounds swell and grow,
And see across the twilight glance,
Troop after troop, in swift advance,
    The shining ones with plumes of snow!

I know the errand of their feet,
    I know what mighty work is theirs;
I can but lift up hands unmeet
The thrashing floors of God to beat,
    And speed them with unworthy prayers.

I will not dream in vain despair,
    The steps of progress wait for me;
The puny leverage of a hair
The planet's impulse well may spare,
    A drop of dew the tided sea.

The loss, if loss there be, is mine;
    And yet not mine if understood;
For one shall grasp and one resign,
One drink life's rue, and one its wine,
    And God shall make the balance good.

O, power to do! O, baffled will!
    O, prayer and action! ye are one.
Who may not strive may yet fulfill
The harder task of standing still,
    And good but wished with God is done!

A MATCH.

BY ALGERNON CHARLES SWINBURNE.

This poem is an excellent example of Swinburne's wonderful invent-
iveness in the meter of his verses.

If love were what the rose is,
And I were like the leaf,
Our lives would grow together
In sad or singing weather,
Blown fields or flowerful closes,
Green pleasure or gray grief;
If love were what the rose is,
And I were like the leaf.

If you were thrall to sorrow,
And I were page to joy,
We'd play for lives and seasons
With loving looks and treasons
And tears of night and morrow
And laughs of maid and boy;
If you were thrall to sorrow,
And I were page to joy.

If you were April's lady,
And I were lord in May,
We'd throw with leaves for hours
And draw for days with flowers,
Till day, like night, were shady,
And night were bright like day;
If you were April's lady,
And I were lord in May.

If you were queen of pleasure,
And I were king of pain,
We'd hunt down love together,
Pluck out his flying feather,
And teach his feet a measure,
And find his mouth a rein;
If you were queen of pleasure,
And I were king of pain.

COUNSEL TO VIRGINS.

BY ROBERT HERRICK.

The advice contained in this poem is not given so subtly nor so gracefully as it is in the other two poems of the trio—Ronsard's and Waller's— but the writer is neither a sweet singer like Ronsard nor a poet of nicer instincts like Waller. He was a man who did not scruple to "sully the purity of his style with impurity of sentiment."

Gather ye rosebuds while ye may,
    Old Time is still a-flying;
And this same flower that smiles to-day
    To-morrow will be dying.

The glorious lamp of Heaven, the sun,
    The higher he's a-getting
The sooner will his race be run,
    And nearer he's to setting.

The age is best which is the first,
  When youth and blood are warmer;
But being spent, the worse and worst
  Times still succeed the former.

Then be not coy, but use your time,
  And, while ye may, go marry;
For having lost but once your prime,
  You may forever tarry.

WHY SO PALE AND WAN?

BY SIR JOHN SUCKLING.

Sir John Suckling was born in Whitton in 1609. He went to Trinity
College, Cambridge, and afterwards entered the service of the King,
Charles I. He fought in the army of Gustavus Adolphus in 1631-'32;
while in 1639 he levied a troop of horse against the Covenanters. He
was a member of the long parliament in 1640. The next year he was
charged with high treason and fled to Paris, where he was supposed to
have committed suicide in 1642. Though he wrote several plays, he is
chiefly noted for his poems.

Why so pale and wan, fond lover?
  Prithee, why so pale?
Will, when looking well can't move her,
  Looking ill prevail?
  Prithee, why so pale?

Why so dull and mute, young sinner?
  Prithee, why so mute?
Will, when speaking well can't win her,
  Saying nothing do't?
  Prithee, why so mute?

Quit, quit, for shame; this will not move;
  This cannot take her.
If of herself she will not love,
  Nothing can make her;
  The devil take her!

THALASSA! THALASSA!

BY BROWNLEE BROWN.

Of this poem Thomas Wentworth Higginson says (in the Outlook,
February, 1890): "It is so magnificent that it cheapens most of its con-
temporary literature, and is alone worth a life otherwise obscure. When
all else of American literature has vanished, who knows but that some
single masterpiece like this may remain to show the high water mark
not merely of a poet but of a nation and a civilization?"

I stand upon the summit of my life,
Behind, the camp, the court, the field, the grove,
The battle, and the burden: vast, afar
Beyond these weary ways, behold, the Sea!
The sea, o'erswept by clouds, and winds, and wings;
By thoughts and wishes manifold; whose breath
Is freshness, and whose mighty pulse is peace.

Palter no question of the horizon dim —
Cut loose the bark! Such voyage itself is rest;
Majestic motion, unimpeded scope,
A widening heaven, a current without care,
Eternity! Deliverance, promise, course,
Time tired souls salute thee from the shore.

AN INDIAN SERENADE.

BY PERCY BYSSHE SHELLEY.

Percy Bysshe Shelley was born in Sussex, England, in 1792. He was educated at Eton and later at University College, Oxford. When he was 19 Shelley married Harriet Westbrook, but after meeting Mary Wollstonecraft he left Harriet and went to Switzerland with Mary. Harriet drowned herself in 1816, and Shelley married Mary. In 1818 they went to Italy, where they lived, for the rest of Shelley's life, with Byron, Trelawney, Edward Williams, and Hunt. Shelley and Williams were drowned in the bay of Spezzia in 1822, and their bodies were burned on a funeral pyre.

I arise from dreams of thee
  In the first sweet sleep of night,
When the winds are breathing low
  And the stars are shining bright.
I arise from dreams of thee,
  And a spirit in my feet
Hath led me—who knows how?
  To thy chamber window, Sweet!

The wandering airs they faint
  In the dark, the silent stream—
And the champak odors pine
  Like sweet thoughts in a dream;
The nightingale's complaint
  It dies upon her heart,
As I must die on thine,
  Oh, belovèd as thou art!

Oh, lift me from the grass!
  I die! I faint! I fail!
Let thy love in kisses rain
  On my lips and eyelids pale.

    My cheek is cold and white, alas!
      My heart beats loud and fast;
    Oh, press it to thine own again,
      Where it will break at last!

THE FOUNT OF CASTALY.

BY JOSEPH O'CONNOR.

Joseph O'Connor was born at Tribes Hill, N. Y., in 1841. He is a graduate of Rochester university, and was admitted to the bar, but never practiced. He taught for a while at the Rochester free academy, but soon left this work for journalism and became editor of the Rochester Post and Express. His poems were published in 1895.

I would the fount of Castaly
   Had never wet my lips;
For woe to him that hastily
   Its sacred water sips.

Apollo's laurel flourishes
   Above that stream divine;
Its secret virtue nourishes
   The leaves of love and wine.

   *   *   *   *

Its joyous tide leaps crystally
   Up 'neath the crystal moon,
And falling ever mistily
   The sparkling drops keep tune.

The wavelets circle gleamingly,
   With lilies keeping trysts;
The emeralds glisten dreamily
   Below, and amethysts.

Once taste that fountain's witchery
   On old Parnassus' crown,
And to this world of treachery
   O, never more come down!

Your joy will be to think of it,
   'Twill ever haunt your dreams;
You'll thirst again to drink of it,
   Among a thousand streams.

THE ROSE.

BY PIERRE RONSARD.

This poem of Pierre Ronsard (1512) is given a place here, as it is an example of that theme which is as old as love or life—the decay of youth and beauty—a subject which has been a favorite with poets in all times. The motive of this little lyric is that of Waller's "Go, Lovely Rose," and of Herrick's "Gather Ye Rosebuds While Ye May."

Come, my Mignonne, let us go—
  Let us see if yonder rose,
  That this morning did disclose
  Robes of crimson to the sun,
  Now that evening has begun,
Still with tints like yours does glow.

Ah, my Mignonne, look and see—
  Look there, underneath the bough;
  Short the space from then till now,
  But its beauties all are past!
  Scarce from morn till eve they last—
Such is nature's harsh decree.

    Ah, my Mignonne, trust to me;
     While your youth as yet is seen
     In its freshest, fairest green,
     Seize the moments to enjoy;
     Old age hastens to destroy
    Roses, beauty, youth, and thee.

FAITH.

BY THOMAS CHATTERTON.

Thomas Chatterton was born in Bristol, England, Nov. 20, 1752. He
ended his life by taking arsenic in a lodging room in London, Aug. 24,
1770. He received a meager education at a charity school in his native
city, began to write verses when he was 12 years old, and at 15 was
apprenticed to a Bristol attorney. He went to London in April, 1770.
He tried to make a living by writing for the newspapers, but failed,
and, reduced to extreme destitution, committed suicide. His Rowley
poems, which he said were translations from the writings of a monk
of the fifteenth century, have been the subject of much discussion.
Besides those he wrote "The Tragedy of Aella," "The Battle of Hast-
ings," "The Tournament," and several shorter poems. His correspond-
ence with Horace Walpole proved a bitter experience for the precocious
poet, who wrote some savage lines on that nobleman author.

O God, whose thunder shakes the sky,
    Whose eye this atom globe surveys,
To thee, my only rock, I fly,
    Thy mercy in thy justice praise.

The mystic mazes of thy will,
    The shadows of celestial light,
Are past the power of human skill;
    But what the Eternal acts is right.

Oh, teach me in the trying hour,
    When anguish swells the dewy tear,
To still my sorrows, own thy power,
    Thy goodness love, thy justice fear.

If in this bosom aught but thee
    Encroaching sought a boundless sway,
Omniscience could the danger see,
    And Mercy look the cause away.

Then why, my soul, dost thou complain,
    Why drooping seek the dark recess?
Shake off the melancholy chain,
    For God created all to bless.

But ah! my breast is human still;
    The rising sigh, the falling tear,
My languid vitals' feeble rill,
    The sickness of my soul declare.

But yet, with fortitude resigned,
   I'll thank the inflicter of the blow;
Forbid the sigh, compose my mind,
   Nor let the gush of misery flow.

The gloomy mantle of the night,
   Which on my sinking spirit steals,
Will vanish at the morning light,
   Which God, my east, my sun, reveals.

THE SONG OF THE CAMP.

BY BAYARD TAYLOR.

Bayard Taylor was born in Pennsylvania in 1825. He was connected with the New York Tribune 1849-'50. Most of his life was spent in travel. In 1853 he joined Perry's expedition to Japan. He corresponded with the American papers, and on his return to this country he lectured. From 1862-'63 he lived at St. Petersburg as Secretary of the Legation there. He died in Berlin, where he was United States Minister, in 1878. He has written of his travels, has translated Goethe's "Faust," and was besides a poet and novelist.

"Give us a song!" the soldiers cried,
    The outer trenches guarding,
When the heated guns of the camps allied
    Grew weary of bombarding.

The dark Redan, in silent scoff,
    Lay grim and threatening under;
And the tawny mound of the Malakoff
    No longer belch'd its thunder.

There was a pause. A guardsman said:
    "We storm the forts tomorrow;
Sing while we may, another day
    Will bring enough of sorrow."

They lay along the battery's side,
    Below the smoking cannon;
Brave hearts from Severn and from Clyde
    And from the banks of Shannon.

They sang of love and not of fame;
    Forgot was Britain's glory;
Each heart recalled a different name,
    But all sang "Annie Laurie."

Voice after voice caught up the song,
    Until its tender passion
Rose like an anthem, rich and strong—
    Their battle-eve confession.

Dear girl, her name he dared not speak,
    But as the song grew louder,
Something upon the soldier's cheek
    Washed off the stains of powder.

Beyond the darkening ocean burned
    The bloody sunset's embers,
While the Crimean valleys learn'd
    How English love remembers.

And once again a fire of hell
    Rain'd on the Russian quarters,
With scream of shot and burst of shell,
    And bellowing of the mortars!

An Irish Nora's eyes are dim
    For a singer dumb and gory;
An English Mary mourns for him
    Who sang of "Annie Laurie."

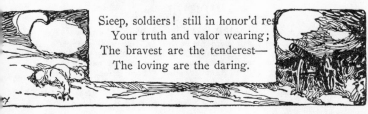

Sleep, soldiers! still in honor'd rest
    Your truth and valor wearing;
The bravest are the tenderest—
    The loving are the daring.

UPHILL.

BY CHRISTINA GEORGINA ROSSETTI.

Christina Rossetti was born at London in 1828. She came of that versatile family, in which the father and sons as well as the daughter were writers, artists, critics and poets. While still in her teens, Miss Rossetti published a little volume called "Maud, Prose and Verse," and crude and morbid as the work was it gave promise of better things. She wrote later, "Goblin Market" (which Dante Gabriel Rossetti illustrated), "A Pageant and Other Poems," and several religious studies. She died in 1894.

Does the road wind uphill all the way?
  Yes, to the very end.
Will the day's journey take the whole long day?
  From morn to night, my friend.

But is there for the night a resting-place?
    A roof for when the slow, dark hours begin.
May not the darkness hide it from my face?
    You cannot miss that inn.

Shall I meet other wayfarers at night?
    Those who have gone before.
Then must I knock, or call when just in sight?
    They will not keep you standing at that door.

Shall I find·comfort, travel-sore and weak?
    Of labour you shall find the sum.
Will there be beds for me and all who seek?
    Yea, beds for all who come.

DOUGLAS, DOUGLAS, TENDER AND TRUE.
BY MISS MULOCK.

Mrs. Craik, better known as Dinah Maria Mulock, was born at Stoke-Upon-Trent, England, 1828, and died at Shortlands, Kent, October 12, 1887. She was the author of many popular novels. She published a volume of poems in 1859, and "Thirty Years' Poems" in 1881, besides many children's books, fairy tales, etc. She married George Lillie Craik, Jr., in 1865.

Could ye come back to me, Douglas, Douglas,
    In the old likeness that I knew,
I would be so faithful, so loving, Douglas,
    Douglas, Douglas, tender and true.

Never a scornful word should grieve ye,
    I'd smile on ye sweet as the angels do—
Sweet as your smile on me shone ever,
    Douglas, Douglas, tender and true.

O, to call back the days that are not!
  My eyes were blinded, your words were few;
Do you know the truth now, up in heaven?
  Douglas, Douglas, tender and true?

I never was worthy of you, Douglas,
  Not half worthy the like of you;
Now, all men beside seem to me like shadows—
  I love you, Douglas, tender and true.

Stretch out your hand to me, Douglas, Douglas,
  Drop forgiveness from heaven like dew,
As I lay my heart on your dead heart, Douglas,
  Douglas, Douglas, tender and true.

TEARS, IDLE TEARS.

BY ALFRED TENNYSON.

This song is found in the "Princess." It was sung on the memorable occasion when the three disguised youths are discovered.

Tears, idle tears, I know not what they mean,
Tears from the depth of some divine despair
Rise in the heart, and gather to the eyes,
In looking on the happy Autumn-fields,
And thinking of the days that are no more.

Fresh as the first beam glittering on a sail,
That brings our friends up from the underworld,
Sad as the last which reddens over one
That sinks with all we love below the verge;
So sad, so fresh, the days that are no more.

Ah, sad and strange as in dark summer dawns
The earliest pipe of half-awaken'd birds
To dying ears when unto dying eyes
The casement slowly grows a glimmering square;
So sad, so strange, the days that are no more.

Dear as remembered kisses after death,
And sweet as those by hopeless fancy feign'd
On lips that are for others; deep as love,
Deep as first love, and wild with all regret;
O, death in life, the days that are no more.

HIGHLAND MARY.

BY ROBERT BURNS.

Ye banks, and braes, and streams around
  The castle o' Montgomery,
Green be your woods, and fair your flowers,
  Your waters never drumlie!
There simmer first unfauld her robes,
  And there the langest tarry!
For there I took the last fareweel
  O' my sweet Highland Mary.

How sweetly bloomed the gay green birk,
  How rich the hawthorn's blossom,
As underneath their fragrant shade
  I clasped her to my bosom!.

The golden hours on angel wings
  Flew o'er me and my dearie;
For dear to me as light and life
  Was my sweet Highland Mary.

Wi' monie a vow and locked embrace
  Our parting was fu' tender;
And, pledging aft to meet again,
  We tore ourselves asunder;
But O! fell death's untimely frost,
  That nipped my flower sae early!
Now green's the sod, and cauld's the clay,
  That wraps my Highland Mary.

O pale, pale now those rosy lips
  I aft hae kissed sae fondly!
And closed for aye the sparkling glance
  That dwelt on me sae kindly!
And mould'ring now in silent dust
  That heart that lo'ed me dearly!
But still within my bosom's core
  Shall live my Highland Mary.

THE LAMB.

BY WILLIAM BLAKE.

In speaking of William Blake's "Songs of Innocence," Swinburne says: "These poems are really unequaled of their kind. Such verse was never written for children since verse writing began.

Little lamb, who made thee?
Dost thou know who made thee,
Gave thee life and bade thee feed
By the stream and o'er the mead;
Gave thee clothing of delight,

153

Softest clothing, woolly, bright;
Gave thee such a tender voice,
Making all the vales rejoice?
Little lamb, who made thee?
Dost thou know who made thee?

Little lamb, I'll tell thee;
Little lamb, I'll tell thee:
He is called by thy name,
For he calls himself a lamb.
He is meek and he is mild,
He became a little child.
I a child, and thou a lamb,
We are called by his name.
Little lamb, God bless thee!
Little lamb, God bless thee!

PSALM XXIV.

The earth is the Lord's, and the fullness thereof;
The world and they that dwell therein.
For he hath founded it upon the seas,
And established it upon the floods.
Who shall ascend into the hill of the Lord?
Or who shall stand in his holy place?
He that hath clean hands,
And a pure heart;
Who hath not lifted up his soul unto vanity,
Nor sworn deceitfully.
He shall receive the blessing from the Lord,
And righteousness from the God of his salvation.
This is the generation of them that seek him,
That seek thy face, O Jacob.
Lift up your heads, O ye gates;
And be ye lift up, ye everlasting doors; and the King of glory
        shall come in.
Who is this King of glory?
The Lord strong and mighty, the Lord mighty in battle.
Lift up your heads, O ye gates;
Even lift them up, ye everlasting doors; and the King of glory
        shall come in.
Who is this King of glory?
The Lord of hosts, he is the King of glory.

SELF-DEPENDENCE.

BY MATTHEW ARNOLD.

Weary of myself, and sick of
    asking
What I am, and what I ought to
    be,
At the vessel's prow I stand,
    which bears me
Forwards, forwards, o'er the
    starlit sea.

And a look of passionate desire
O'er the sea and to the stars I
    send;
"Ye, who from my childhood up
    have claimed me,
Calm me, ah, compose me to the
    end!

"Ah, once more," I cried, "ye
    stars, ye waters,
On my heart your mighty charm
    renew;
Still, still let me, as I gaze upon
    you,
Feel my soul becoming vast like
    you!"

From the intense, clear, star sown vault of heaven,
O'er the lit sea's unquiet way,
In the rustling night air came the answer—
"Wouldst thou be as these are? Live as they.

"Unaffrighted by the silence round them,
Undistracted by the sights they see,
These demand not that the things without them
Yield them love, amusement, sympathy.

"And with joy the stars perform their shining,
And the sea its long moon silver'd roll;
For self-poised they live, nor pine with noting
All the fever of some differing soul.

"Bounded by themselves, and unregardful
In what state God's other works may be,
In their own tasks all their powers pouring,
These attain the mighty life you see."

O, air born voice! long since, severely clear,
A cry like thine in mine own heart I hear—
"Resolve to be thyself; and know that he
Who finds himself loses his misery!"

THE ARSENAL AT SPRINGFIELD.

BY HENRY W. LONGFELLOW.

Mr. Longfellow and his second wife, during their honeymoon, visited the United States arsenal at Springfield, Mass., about half a century ago. The figure of speech in which the poet speaks of the burnished arms rising like a huge organ was suggested by Mrs. Longfellow. The poem was inspired by Charles Sumner's oration, "The True Grandeur of Nations," which was an argument for peace and against war.

This is the Arsenal. From floor to ceiling,
　　Like a huge organ, rise the burnished arms;
But from their silent pipes no anthem pealing
　　Startles the villages with strange alarms.

Ah, what a sound will rise, how wild and dreary,
　　When the death angel touches those swift keys!
What loud lament and dismal Miserere
　　Will mingle with their awful symphonies!

I hear even now the infinite fierce chorus,
　　The cries of agony, the endless groan,
Which, through the ages that have gone before us,
　　In long reverberations reach our own.

On helm and harness rings the Saxon hammer,
　　Through Cimbric forest roars the Norseman's song,
And loud, amid the universal clamor,
　　O'er distant deserts sounds the Tartar gong.

I hear the Florentine, who from his palace
　　Wheels out his battle bell with dreadful din,
And Aztec priests upon their teocallis
　　Beat the wild war drums made of serpent's skin.

The tumult of each sacked and burning village;
　The shout that every prayer for mercy drowns;
The soldiers' revels in the midst of pillage;
　The wail of famine in beleaguered towns;

The bursting shell, the gateway wrenched asunder,
　The rattling musketry, the clashing blade;
And ever and anon, in tones of thunder,
　The diapason of the cannonade.

Is it, O man, with such discordant noises,
　With such accursed instruments as these,
Thou drownest nature's sweet and kindly voices,
　And jarrest the celestial harmonies?

Were half the power that fills the world with terror,
　Were half the wealth bestowed on camps and courts,
Given to redeem the human mind from error,
　There were no need of arsenals or forts.

The warrior's name would be a name abhorred
　And every nation, that should lift again
Its hand against a brother, on its forehead
　Would wear for evermore the curse of Cain!

Down the dark future, through long generations,
　The echoing sounds grow fainter, and then cease;
And, like a bell, with solemn, sweet vibrations,
　I hear once more the voice of Christ say "Peace!"

Peace! And no longer from its brazen portals
　The blast of war's great organ shakes the skies!
But beautiful as songs of the immortals
　The holy melodies of love arise.

ALL.

BY FRANCIS A. DURIVAGE.

Francis A. Durivage was born at Boston in 1814 and engaged early in journalistic work, writing for the magazines as well. He won considerable reputation with a series of humorous articles signed "Old Un." He wrote a great many poems of serious as well as of light character, and several plays. He published "Cyclopedia of Biography," "The Fatal Casket," "Life Scenes from the World Around Us," was part translator of Lamartine's "History of the Revolution of 1848," and co-author of "Stray Subjects." He died in New York city in 1881.—Bayard Taylor.]

["I know of no finer poem of its length."—Bayard Taylor.]

There hangs a saber, and there a rein,
With a rusty buckle and green curb chain
A pair of spurs on the old gray wall,
And a mouldy saddle—well, that is all.

Come out to the stable—it is not far;
The moss grown door is hanging ajar.
Look within! There's an empty stall,
Where once stood a charger, and that is all.

The good black horse came riderless home,
Flecked with blood drops as well as foam;
See yonder hillock where dead leaves fall
The good black horse pined to death—
            that's all.

All? O, God! it is all I can speak.
Question me not—I am old and weak;
His saber and his saddle hang on the wall
And his horse pined to death—I have told
            you all.

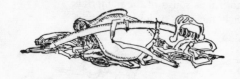

LIFE.

BY MRS. A. L. BARBAULD.

Anna Letitia Barbauld, the daughter of the Rev. John Aiken, was
born at Kilworth-Harcourt, in Leicestershire, 1743. She married the Rev.
Rochemond Barbauld. A poet as well as an essayist, she wrote
"Poems," "Hymns in Prose for Children," "The Female Spectator," and
"Eighteen Hundred and Eleven." She died at Stoke-Newington in 1825.

Life! I know not what thou art,
But know that thou and I must part;
And when, or how, or where we met
I own to me 's a secret yet.

Life! we've been long together
Through pleasant and through cloudy
   weather;
'Tis hard to part when friends are
   dear—
Perhaps 't will cost a sigh, a tear;
Then steal away, give little warning,
 Choose thine own time;
  Say not "Good night," but in some
   brighter clime
Bid me "Good morning."

THE DAFFODILS.

BY WILLIAM WORDSWORTH.

I wandered, lonely as a cloud
  That floats on high o'er vales and hills,
When all at once I saw a crowd,
  A host of golden daffodils,
Beside the lake, beneath the trees,
Fluttering and dancing in the breeze.

Continuous as the stars that shine
  And twinkle on the milky way,
They stretch'd in never-ending line
  Along the margin of a bay;
Ten thousand saw I at a glance
Tossing their heads in sprightly dance.

The waves beside them danced, but they
  Outdid the sparkling waves in glee;
A poet could not but be gay
  In such jocund company!
I gazed—and gazed—but little thought
What wealth to me the show had brought;

For oft, when on my couch I lie
  In vacant or in pensive mood,
They flash upon that inward eye
  Which is the bliss of solitude;
And then my heart with pleasure fills,
And dances with the daffodils.

SONG ON MAY MORNING.

BY JOHN MILTON.

John Milton was born at London in 1608. At 16 he went to Christ's College, Cambridge, and there wrote his "Ode on the Nativity" (1629). During the Long Parliament Milton wrote many political pamphlets attacking the Episcopacy, and later, when Charles I. had been executed, he answered the "Eikon Basilike" of Gauden with his famous "Eikonoclastes." At home Milton suffered through the neglect and impatience of his daughters, who, on account of his blindness, were the unwilling amanuenses, of "Paradise Lost," and "Paradise Regained." Besides these epic poems are "L'Allegro," "Il Penseroso," "Comus," and "Lycidas," all of which were written between 1634-'37. He died in 1674.

Now the bright morning star,
    day's harbinger,
Comes dancing from the East,
    and leads with her
The flowery May, who from
    her green lap throws
The yellow cowslip and the pale
    primrose.
Hail, bounteous May, that doth
    inspire
Mirth and youth and warm desire;
Woods and groves are of thy
    dressing,
Hill and dale doth boast thy
    blessing;
Thus we salute thee with our early
    song,
And welcome thee, and wish thee
    long.

GROUNDS OF THE TERRIBLE.

BY HAROLD BEGBIE.

The death is announced of First Class Petty Officer Grounds of H. M. S. Terrible, the best shot with a heavy gun in the British navy. Grounds' wages were 3 shillings per day, and for the unparalleled achievement of making eight shots in one minute in 1901 with the six-inch gun, and seven hits out of eight rounds in one minute under most unfavorable weather conditions in 1902, he received in all the magnificent remuneration of 1 shilling 9 pence, and 6 shillings 3 pence in the two years, "his proper share of prize money."

The statesman at the council, and the gunner at the breech:
  The hand upon the parchment and the eye along the sight:
O, the cry is on the waters: Have ye weighed the worth of
      each?
  Have ye shown a mandate stronger than ability to smite?

He was the best with a heavy gun in the whole o' the British
    fleet,
And the run of his pay? Three shillin's a day, with biscuit
    and salted meat.
He was the man who could pitch his shell on a mark that was
    never still
Eight times true while a minute flew, and parliament whittled
    the bill;
He was a man who could soothe a gun in the race of a swiriing
    tide,
Who could chime his shots with the charging knots of a ship
    with a dripping side,
Who could get to his mark from a dancing deck that never a
    moment stood,
Content to hear, for a Bisley cheer, a midshipman's muttered
    "Good!"

Never his eye will steady now thro' the spray and the whistling
    rain,
To loose the scream from the foaming lips and splinter the
    mark in twain;
Never again will he win his share in the prize that my lords
    assign—
Six-and-three in a single year, and once—it was one-and-
    nine!

164

Never again! He has fired the last of the shells that the state
 allowed,
He has turned from the roar of the six-inch bore to the hush
 of the hammock shroud,
And never a bell in England tolled, and who was it caught his
 breath
When the Shot o' the Fleet first dipped his feet in the flooding
 ford of Death?

Gladder, I think, would the gunner's soul have passed thro' the
 closing dark
Had he known that ye cared with patriot joy when the navy
 hit the mark;
Gladder, I think, would the gunner's soul have passed to the
 farther shore
Had the Mother Land once gripped his hand, and uttered the
 pride she bore.
Gold is the prize that all men seek, tho' the mark be honor and
 fame;
Declare: Have ye spurned by a gift or a word the Terrible
 gunners' aim?
Will ye care to know what the men can do when the hosts of
 hate embark?
What of your sons at the old sea guns?—have ye cared if they
 hit the mark?

IN THE GRAVEYARD.

BY MACDONALD CLARKE.

Macdonald Clarke was born at New London, Conn., in 1798. On account of his many eccentricities he gained the name of the "Mad Poet." His poems have been collected under the titles of "A Review of the Eve of Eternity and Other Poems," "The Elixir of Moonshine, by the Mad Poet," "The Gossip," "Poetic Sketches," and "The Belles of Broadway." He died in 1842.

'Mid the half-lit air, and the lonely place,
  Rose the buried Pleasures of perish'd years.
I saw the Past, with her pallid face,
  Whose smiles had turned to tears.
On many a burial stone,
I read the names of beings once known,
  Who oft in childish glee,
  Had jumped across the graves with me—
Sported, many a truant day,
Where—now their ashes lay.

There the dead Poet had been placed,
  Who died in the dawn of thought—
And there, the girl whose virtues graced
  The lines his love had wrought—
Beauty's power, and Talent's pride,
  And Passion's fever, early chill'd
  The heart that felt, the eye that thrill'd,
All, the dazzling dreams of each,
Faded, out of Rapture's reach.

O, when they trifled, on this spot,
  Not long ago,
Little they thought, 'twould be their lot,
  So soon to lie here lone and low,
'Neath a chilly coverlid of clay,
  And few or none to go
'Mid the glimmering dusk of a summer day,
To the dim place where they lay,

And pause and pray,
　　And think how little worth,
　　Is all that frets our hearts on earth.

The sun had sunk, and the summer skies
　　Were dotted with specks of light,
That melted soon, in the deep moon-rise,
　　That flowed over Croton Height.
For the Evening, in her robe of white,
　　Smiled o'er sea and land, with pensive eyes,
Saddening the heart, like the first fair night.
　　After a loved one dies.

BONNY DUNDEE.

BY SIR WALTER SCOTT

To the lords of convention 'twas Claver'se who spoke,
"Ere the king's crown shall fall there are crowns to be broke;
So let each cavalier who loves honor and me
Come follow the bonnet of Bonny Dundee.

　　　Come fill up my cup, come fill up my can,
　　　Come saddle your horses, and call up your men;
　　　Come open the West Port and let me gang free,
　　　And it's room for the bonnets of Bonny Dundee."

Dundee he is mounted, he rides up the street,
The bells are rung backward, the drums they are beat;
But the provost, douce man, said, "Just e'en let him be,
The gude town is weel quit of the deil of Dundee."

With sour featured whigs the Grassmarket was crammed,
As if half the west had set tryst to be hanged;
There was spite in each look, there was fear in each ee,
As they watched for the bonnets of Bonny Dundee.

These cowls of Kilmarnock had spits and had spears,
And lang hafted gullies to kill cavaliers;
And they shrunk to close heads, and the causeway was free,
At the toss of the bonnet of Bonny Dundee.

"Away to the hills, to the caves, to the rocks—
Ere I own an usurper, I'll couch with the fox;
And tremble, false whigs, in the midst of your glee;
You have not seen the last of my bonnets and me."

BORDER BALLAD.

BY SIR WALTER SCOTT.

March, march, Ettrick and Teviotdale,
  Why the deil dinna ye march forward in order?
March, march, Eskdale and Liddesdale
  All the Blue Bonnets are bound for the border.
    Many a banner spread
    Flutters above your head,
  Many a crest that is famous in story.
    Mount and make ready then,
    Sons of the mountain glen,
  Fight for the queen and our old Scottish glory.

Come from the hills where your hirsels are grazing,
  Come from the glen of the buck and the roe;
Come to the crag where the beacon is blazing,
  Come with the buckler, the lance, and the bow.
    Trumpets are sounding,
    War steeds are bounding;
  Stand to your arms, then, and march in good order,
    England shall many a day
    Tell of the bloody fray,
  When the Blue Bonnets came over the Border.

TO THE DANDELION.

BY JAMES RUSSELL LOWELL.

This poem, like Bryant's "Waterfowl," like many of Longfellow's, speaks of the objects of nature in a reflective, almost religious tone, portraying the love of our American poets for "these living pages of God's book."

Dear common flower, that grow'st
  beside the way,
  Fringing the dusty road with
    harmless gold,
First pledge of blithesome May,
  Which children pluck, and, full
    of pride, uphold,
High hearted buccaneers,
    o'erjoyed that they
An El Dorado in the grass have
    found,
Which not the rich earth's ample
    round
May match in wealth, thou art
    more dear to me
Than all the prouder summer
    blooms may be.

Gold such as thine ne'er drew the
    Spanish prow
  Through the primeval hush of
    Indian seas,
Nor wrinkled the lean brow
  Of age to rob the lover's heart
    of ease;
Tis the spring's largess, which she scatters now
To rich and poor alike, with lavish hand,
Though most hearts never understand
To take it at God's value, but pass by
The offered wealth with unrewarded eye,

Thou art my tropics and mine Italy;
　To look at thee unlocks a warmer clime;
The eyes thou givest
　Are in the heart, and heed not space or time.
Not in mid-June the gold cuirassed bee
Feels a more summerlike warm ravishment
In the white lily's breezy tent,
His fragrant Sybaris, than I, when first
From the dark green thy yellow circles burst.

How like a prodigal doth nature seem,
　When thou, for all thy gold, so common art!
Thou teachest me to deem
　More sacredly of every human heart,
Since each reflects in joy its scanty gleam
Of heaven, and could some wondrous secret show,
Did we but pay the love we owe.
And with a child's undoubting wisdom look,
On all these pages of God's book.

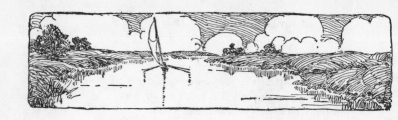

THE BALLAD OF THE BOAT.

BY RICHARD GARNETT.

This poem has passed in American books of selections as having been written by an unknown "R. Garrett," this being mainly the consequence of an error in editing the little book called "Sea and Shore," some twenty years ago. It now, however, appears as the work of a man dear to many Americans, Dr. Richard Garnett, late of the British museum.

The stream was smooth as glass. We said: "Arise, and let's
    away."
The Siren sang beside the boat that in the rushes lay,
And spread the sail and strong the oar, we gayly took our way.
When shall the sandy bar be crost? When shall we find the
    bay?

The broadening flood swells slowly out o'er cattle dotted
    plains;
The stream is strong and turbulent, and dark with heavy rains;
The laborer looks up to see our shallop speed away.
When shall the sandy bar be crost? When shall we find the
    bay?

Now are the clouds like fiery shrouds; the sun, superbly large,
Slow as an oak to woodman's stroke, sinks flaming at their
    marge;
The waves are bright with mirror'd light as jacinths on our
    way.
When shall the sandy bar be crost? When shall we find the
    bay?

The moon is high up in the sky, and now no more we see
The spreading river's either bank, and surging distantly
There booms a sudden thunder as of breakers far away;
Now shall the sandy bar be crost, now shall we find the bay!

The seagull shrieks high overhead, and dimly to our sight
The moonlit crests of foaming waves gleam towering through
        the night.
We'll steal upon the mermaid soon, and start her from her lay,
When once the sandy bar is crost and we are in the bay.

What rises white and awful as a shroud enfolded ghost?
What roar of rampant tumult bursts in clangor on the coast?
Pull back! pull back! The raging flood sweeps every oar away.
O stream, is this thy bar of sand? O boat, is this the bay?

NEARER HOME.

BY PHOEBE CARY.

Phoebe Cary, sister of Alice Cary, was born in Hamilton County, near Cincinnati, Sept. 24, 1824; died in Newport, R. I., July 31, 1871. Her educational advantages were superior to those of Alice, whose constant companion she was through life. "Nearer Home" was written when she was 18 years old. Intense sorrow for her sister, whom she survived, doubtless hastened her death.

One sweetly solemn thought
   Comes to me o'er and o'er;
I'm nearer my home today
   Than I ever have been before;

Nearer my Father's house,
   Where the many mansions be;
Nearer the great white throne,
   Nearer the crystal sea;

Nearer the bound of life,
   Where we lay our burdens down;
Nearer leaving the cross,
   Nearer gaining the crown!

But lying darkly between,
   Winding down through the night,
Is the silent, unknown stream,
   That leads us at length to the light.

Closer and closer my steps
   Come to the dread abysm;
Closer Death to my lips
   Presses the awful chrism.

O, if my mortal feet
   Have almost gained the brink;
If it be I am nearer home
   Even today than I think;

Father, perfect my trust;
   Let my spirit feel in death
That her feet are firmly set
   On the rock of a living faith!

THE TIGER.

BY WILLIAM BLAKE.

William Blake was born at London in 1757; he died there in 1827. He is well known among children for his "Songs of Innocence." Other of his works are: "Book of Thel," the "Marriage of Heaven and Earth," "Gates of Paradise," "Songs of Experience." He was also a painter and an engraver, and among his best work in that line are his illustrations to Blair's "Grave," and to the book of Job.

Tiger, tiger, burning bright
In the forests of the night,
What immortal hand or eye
Could frame thy fearful symmetry?

In what distant deeps or skies
Burnt the fire of thine eyes?
On what wings dare he aspire?
What the hand dare seize the fire?

And what shoulder and what art
Could twist the sinews of thine heart?
And when thy heart began to beat,
What dread hand and what dread feet?

What the hammer? What the chain?
In what furnace was thy brain?
What the anvil? What dread grasp
Dare its deadly terrors clasp?

When the stars threw down their spears,
And water'd heaven with their tears,
Did he smile his work to see?
Did he who made the lamb make thee?

Tiger, tiger, burning bright
In the forests of the night,
What immortal hand or eye
Dare frame thy fearful symmetry?

ANNABEL LEE.

BY EDGAR ALLAN POE.

It was many and many a year ago,
   In a kingdom by the sea,
That a maiden lived whom you may know
   By the name of Annabel Lee;
And this maiden she lived with no other thought
   Than to love and be loved by me.

I was a child and she was a child,
   In this kingdom by the sea;
But we loved with a love that was more than love,
   I and my Annabel Lee;
With a love that the winged seraphs of heaven
   Coveted her and me.

And this was the reason that long ago,
   In this kingdom by the sea,
A wind blew out of a cloud, chilling
   My beautiful Annabel Lee;
So that her high born kinsman came
   And bore her away from me,
To shut her up in a sepulcher
   In this kingdom by the sea.

The angels, not so happy in heaven,
   Went envying her and me;
Yes! that was the reason (as all men know,
   In this kingdom by the sea)
That the wind came out of the cloud by night,
   Chilling and killing my Annabel Lee.

But our love it was stronger by far than the love
    Of those who were older than we,
    Of many far wiser than we;
And neither the angels in heaven above,
    Nor the demons down under the sea,
Can ever dissever my soul from the soul
    Of the beautiful Annabel Lee.

For the moon never beams without bringing me dreams
    Of the beautiful Annabel Lee;
And the stars never rise but I feel the bright eyes
    Of the beautiful Annabel Lee;
And so, all the night tide, I lie down by the side
Of my darling—my darling—my life and my bride,
    In her sepulcher there by the sea,
    In her tomb by the sounding sea.

TODAY.
BY THOMAS CARLYLE.

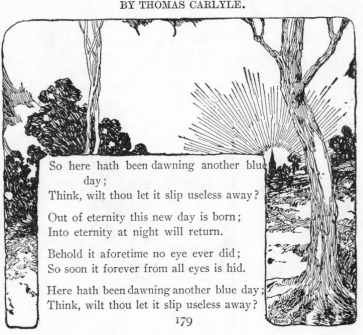

So here hath been dawning another blue
    day;
Think, wilt thou let it slip useless away?

Out of eternity this new day is born;
Into eternity at night will return.

Behold it aforetime no eye ever did;
So soon it forever from all eyes is hid.

Here hath been dawning another blue day;
Think, wilt thou let it slip useless away?

179

MY BOAT IS ON THE SHORE

BY LORD BYRON.

My boat is on the shore,
　And my bark is on the sea;
But before I go, Tom Moore,
　Here's a double health to thee!

Here's a sigh to those who love me,
　And a smile to those who hate;
And, whatever sky's above me,
　Here's a heart for every fate!

Though the ocean roar around me,
　Yet it still shall bear me on;
Though a desert should surround me,
　It hath springs that may be won.

Were't the last drop in the well,
　As I gasp'd upon the brink,
Ere my fainting spirit fell,
　'T is to thee that I would drink.

With that water, as this wine,
　The libation I would pour
Should be—Peace with thine and mine,
　And a health to thee, Tom Moore!

INDIAN SUMMER.

BY JOHN GREENLEAF WHITTIER.

From gold to gray
Our mild, sweet day
Of Indian summer fades too soon;
But tenderly
Above the sea
Hangs, white and calm, the hunter's moon.

In its pale fire
The village spire
Shows like the zodiac's spectral lance;
The painted walls
Whereon it falls
Transfigured stand in marble trance!

SCOTS WHA HAE.

BY ROBERT BURNS.

A friend of Burns states this stirring poem was written during a frightful storm in the wilds of Glenken, in Galloway. It was written in September, 1793.

Scots, wha hae wi' Wallace bled,
Scots, wham Bruce has often led;
Welcome to your gory bed,
   Or to victorie!

Now's the day, and now's the hour;
See the front o' battle lour;
See approach proud Edward's pow'r—
   Chains and slaverie!

Wha will be a traitor-knave?
Wha can fill a coward's grave?
Wha sae base as be a slave?
   Let him turn and flee!

Wha for Scotland's king and law
Freedom's sword will strongly draw,
Freeman stand, or freeman fa',
   Let him follow me!

By oppression's woes and pains!
By our sons in servile chains!
We will drain our dearest veins,
   But they shall be free!

Lay the proud usurpers low!
Tyrants fall in every foe!
Liberty's in every blow!
   Let us do or die!

JERUSALEM, THE GOLDEN.

TRANSLATED FROM THE LATIN, BY JOHN M. NEALE.

Jerusalem, the golden,
  With milk and honey blest!
Beneath thy contemplation
  Sink heart and voice oppressed;
I know not, Oh, I know not,
  What joys await me there,
What radiancy of glory,
  What bliss beyond compare.

They stand, those halls of Zion,
  All jubilant with song,
And bright with many an angel,
  And all the martyr throng;
The Prince is ever in them,
  The daylight is serene;
The pastures of the blessed
  Are decked in glorious sheen.

There is the throne of David;
  And there, from care released,
The shout of them that triumph,
  The song of them that feast:
And they who, with their Leader,
  Have conquered in the fight
Forever and forever
  Are clad in robes of white.

MISCONCEPTIONS.

BY ROBERT BROWNING.

This is a spray the Bird clung to,
Making it blossom with pleasure,
Ere the high tree-top she sprung to,
Fit for her nest and her treasure.
Oh, what a hope beyond measure
Was the poor spray's which the flying feet hung
    to,—
So to be singled out, built in and sung to!

This is a heart the Queen leant on
Thrilled in a minute erratic,
Ere the true bosom she bent on,
Meet for love's regal dalmatic.
Oh what a fancy ecstatic
Was the poor heart's, ere the wanderer went
    on—
Love to be saved for it, proffered to, spent on!

JOHN ANDERSON, MY JO.

BY ROBERT BURNS.

John Anderson, my jo, John,
  When we were first acquent,
Your locks were like the raven,
  Your bonny brow was brent;
But now your brow is beld, John,
  Your locks are like the snaw;
But blessings on your frosty pow,
  John Anderson, my jo.

John Anderson, my jo, John,
  We clamb the hill thegither;
And monie a canty day, John,
  We've had wi' ane anither.
Now we maun totter down, John,
  But hand in hand we'll go,
And sleep thegither at the foot,
  John Anderson, my jo.

MAID OF ATHENS, ERE WE PART.

BY LORD BYRON.

Zoe mou sas agapo.
(My life, I love thee.)

Maid of Athens, ere we part,
Give, oh, give me back my heart!
Or, since that has left my breast,
Keep it now and take the rest!
Hear my vow before I go,
Zoè mou sas agapo.

By those tresses unconfined,
Woo'd by each Ægean wind;
By those lids whose jetty fringe
Kiss thy soft cheeks' blooming tinge;
By those wild eyes like the roe,
Zoè mou sas agapo.

By that lip I long to taste;
By that zone-encircled waist;
By all the token-flowers that tell
What words can never speak so well;
By love's alternate joy and woe,
Zoè mou sas agapo.

Maid of Athens! I am gone:
Think of me, sweet! when alone.
Though I fly to Istambol,
Athens holds my heart and soul:
Can I cease to love thee? No!
Zoè mou sas agapo.

TO CELIA.

BEN JONSON.

Ben Jonson was born about the year 1573, at Westminster. Little is known about his early life, but in 1597 he is found playing and writing for "The Admiral's Men," and later for the "Lord Chamberlain's Servants." Afterwards he stood in great favor at court, and wrote many of his best plays during that time—the "Alchemist," "Catiline," "Bartholomew Fair," and "Epicoene." He died in 1637, after several years of illness, which affected his wit and brilliancy in such a manner that many of his later plays were not heard to the end. He is buried in Westminster Abbey. He also wrote some prose and some of the most beautiful lyrics of the English language.

Drink to me only with thine eyes,
  And I will pledge with mine;
Or leave a kiss but in the cup
  And I'll not look for wine.
The thirst that from the soul
    doth rise
  Doth ask a drink divine;
But might I of Jove's nectar sup,
  I would not change for thine.

I sent thee late a rosy wreath,
  Not so much honoring thee
As giving it a hope that there
  It could not withered be;
  But thou thereon didst only
    breathe
  And sent'st it back to me;
Since when it grows, and smells,
    I swear,
  Not of itself but thee.

A LOVER'S QUARREL

BY AUSTIN DOBSON.

NELLIE.

If I were you, when ladies at the play, sir,
 Beckon and nod, a melodrama through,
I would not turn abstractedly away, sir,
  If I were you!

FRANK.

If I were you, when persons I affected,
 Wait for three hours to take me down to Kew,
I would, at least, pretend I recollected,
  If I were you!

NELLIE.

If I were you, when ladies are so lavish,
      Sir, as to keep me every waltz but two,
I would not dance with odious Miss McTavish,
      If I were you!

FRANK.

If I were you, who vow you cannot suffer
      Whiff of the best—the mildest "honey-dew,"
I would not dance with smoke-consuming Puffer,
      If I were you!

NELLIE.

If I were you, I would not, sir, be bitter,
      Even to write the "Cynical Review"——

FRANK.

No, I should doubtless find flirtation fitter,
      If I were you!

NELLIE.

Really! You would? Why, Frank, you're quite delightful—
      Hot as Othello, and as black of hue;
Borrow my fan. I would not look so frightful,
      If I were you!

FRANK.

"It is the cause." I mean your chaperon is
      Bringing some well-curled juvenile. Adieu!
I shall retire. I'd spare that poor Adonis,
      If I were you!

NELLIE.

Go, if you will. At once! And by express, sir!
      Where shall it be? to China—or Peru?
Go. I should leave inquirers my address, sir,
      If I were you!

FRANK.

No—I remain. To stay and fight a duel
  Seems on the whole, the proper thing to do—
Ah, you are strong—I would not then be cruel,
  If I were you!

NELLIE.

One does not like one's feelings to be doubted—

FRANK.

One does not like one's friends to misconstrue—

NELLIE.

If I confess that I a wee-bit pouted?

FRANK.

I should admit that I was piqued, too.

NELLIE.

Ask me to dance! I'd say no more about it,
  If I were you!

    (Waltz—Exeunt.)

KUBLA KHAN

BY SAMUEL T. COLERIDGE.

Samuel Taylor Coleridge was born at Ottery St. Mary, Devonshire 1772. He studied at Cambridge, but left without taking his degree. In 1795 he married Sara Fricker, Southey's sister-in-law; in the same year he moved to Bristol. Here he published, in collaboration with Words-worth, the "Lyrical Ballads." In 1798 he went to Germany on an annuity from the Wedgewood brothers, but he soon returned to England and lived at Keswick. Later he went to London, where he lived at the house of Dr. Gilman and lectured on Shakespeare and the fine arts. He died at London in 1834.

In Xanadu did Kubla Khan
  A stately pleasure dome decree,
Where Alph, the sacred river, ran,
Through caverns measureless to man,
  Down to a sunless sea.
So twice five miles of fertile ground

With walls and towers were
    girdled round;
And there were gardens bright
    with sinuous rills,
    Where blossomed many an
    incense bearing tree;
And here were forests ancient as
    the hills,
    Enfolding sunny spots of
    greenery.
The shadow of the dome of
    pleasure
    Floated midway on the
    waves,
Where was heard the mingled
    measure
    From the fountain and the
    caves.
It was a miracle of rare device,
A sunny pleasure dome with
    caves of ice!
    A damsel with a dulcimer
    In a vision once I saw;
It was an Abyssinian maid,
    And on her dulcimer she played,
Singing of Mount Abora.
Could I revive within me
    Her symphony and song
To such deep delight 'twould win me
  That with music loud and long
I would build that dome in air—
    That sunny dome! those caves of ice!
And all who heard should see them there,
And all should cry, Beware! Beware!
His flashing eyes, his floating hair!
    Weave a circle round him thrice,
And close your eyes with holy dread,
For he on honey dew hath fed
    And drunk the milk of Paradise.

A BALLAD UPON A WEDDING.

BY SIR JOHN SUCKLING.

Her finger was so small, the ring
Would not stay on, which they did bring,
   It was too wide a peck;
And to say truth (for out it must),
It looked like the great collar (just)
   About our young colt's neck.

Her feet beneath her petticoat,
Like little mice, stole in and out,
   As if they fear'd the light;
But oh, she dances such a way!
No sun upon an Easter day
   Is half so fine a sight.

Her cheeks so rare a white was on,
No daisy makes comparison,
   (Who sees them is undone),
For streaks of red were mingled there,
Such as are on a Catherine pear
   (The side that's next the sun).

Her lips were red, and one was thin,
Compar'd to that was next her chin
   (Some bee had stung it newly);
But (Dick) her eyes so guard her face
I durst no more upon them gaze
   Than on the sun in July.

CROSSING THE BAR.

BY ALFRED TENNYSON.

Sunset and evening star
    And one clear call for me!
And may there be no moaning of the bar,
    When I put out to sea.

But such a tide as moving seems asleep,
    Too full for sound and foam,
When that which drew from out the boundless deep
    Turns again home.

Twilight and evening bell,
    And after that the dark!
And may there be no sadness of farewell,
    When I embark;

For tho' from out our bourne of Time and Place
    The flood may bear me far,
I hope to see my Pilot face to face
    When I have crossed the bar.

JUNE.

BY JAMES RUSSELL LOWELL.

And what is so rare as a day in June?
    Then, if ever, come perfect days;
Then heaven tries the earth if it be in tune,
    And over it softly her warm ear lays;
Whether we look, or whether we listen,
    We hear life murmur, or see it glisten;
Every clod feels a stir of might,
    An instinct within it that reaches and towers,
And, groping blindly above it for light,
    Climbs to a soul in grass and flowers;
The flush of life may well be seen
    Thrilling back over hills and valleys;
The cowslip startles in meadows green,
    The buttercup catches the sun in its chalice,

And there's never a leaf nor a blade too mean
    To be some happy creature's palace;
The little bird sits at his door in the sun,
    Atilt like a blossom among the leaves,
And lets his illumined being o'errun
    With the deluge of summer it receives;
His mate feels the eggs beneath her wings,
And the heart in her dumb breast flutters and sings
He sings to the wide world and she to her nest—
In the nice ear of nature, which song is the best?

THE HARP THAT ONCE THROUGH TARA'S HALLS.
BY THOMAS MOORE.

The harp that once through Tara's halls
    The soul of music shed,
Now hangs as mute on Tara's walls
    As if that soul were fled.
So sleeps the pride of former days,
    So glory's thrill is o'er,
And hearts that once beat high for praise
    Now feel that pulse no more.

No more to chiefs and ladies bright
    The harp of Tara swells;
The chord alone that breaks at night
    Its tale of ruin tells.
Thus Freedom now so seldom wakes,
    The only throb she gives,
Is when some heart indignant breaks,
    To show that still she lives

THE BELLS OF SHANDON.

BY FRANCIS MAHONY.

Francis Sylvester Mahony, better known as Father Prout, was born in Cork in 1804. Though he was a Jesuit priest, he was more of a literatus than a man of God. He is the author of the famous "Reliques of Father Prout," which he wrote for Frazer's Magazine. Later he was the Rome correspondent for the Daily News and the Paris correspondent of the Globe. He died in Paris in 1866. Among his poems the following is the only one worth mention:

With deep affection and recollection
    I often think of those Shandon bells,
Whose sounds so wild would in the days of childhood
    Fling round my cradle their magic spells.
    On this I ponder, where'er I wander,
And thus grow fonder, sweet Cork, of thee;
        With thy bells of Shandon,
        That sound so grand on
The pleasant waters of the River Lee.

I have heard bells chiming full many a clime in,
　　Tolling sublime in cathedral shrine;
While at a glib rate brass tongues would vibrate,
　　But all their music spoke naught like thine;
　　For memory dwelling on each proud swelling
Of thy belfry knelling its bold notes free,
　　　　Made the bells of Shandon
　　　　Sound far more grand on
The pleasant waters of the River Lee.

I have heard bells tolling "old Adrian's mole" in,
　　Their thunder rolling from the Vatican,
And cymbals glorious, swinging uproarious,
　　In the gorgeous turrets of Notre Dame;
　　But thy sounds were sweeter than the dome of Peter
Flings o'er the Tiber, pealing solemnly.
　　　　O! the bells of Shandon
　　　　Sound far more grand on
The pleasant waters of the River Lee.

There's a bell in Moscow, while on tower and kiosko
　　In St. Sophia the Turkman gets,
And loud in air calls men to prayer
　　From the tapering summit of tall minarets.
　　Such empty phantom I freely grant 'em,
But there's an anthem more dear to me;
　　　　'Tis the bells of Shandon,
　　　　That sound so grand on
The pleasant waters of the River Lee.

THE GARRET.

BY W. M. THACKERAY.

The many theater-goers who were pleased with Mr. Esmond's comedy, "When We Were Twenty-One," as played by the Goodwins, may like to see the Thackeray song from which the play took its name. It is an imitation of a poem by Beranger.

With pensive eyes the little room
I view,
Where in my youth I
weathered it so long,
With a wild mistress, a stanch
friend or two,
And a light heart still
breaking into song;
Making a mock of life and all its
cares,
Rich in the glory of my rising
sun,
Lightly I vaulted up four pair
of stairs,
In the brave days when I was
twenty-one.

Yes, 'tis a garret, let him know't
who will;
There was my bed—full hard
it was and small;
My table there—and I decipher
still
Half a lame couplet
charcoaled on the wall.

Ye joys that Time hath swept with him away,
Come to mine eyes, ye dreams of love and fun
For you I pawned my watch how many a day,
In the brave days when I was twenty-one.

*   *   *   *   *   *

One jolly evening, when my friends and I
　　Made happy music with our songs and cheers,
A shout of triumph mounted up thus high,
　　And distant cannon opened on our ears;
We rise—we join in the triumphant strain—
　　Napoleon conquers—Austerlitz is won—
Tyrants shall never tread us down again,
　　In the brave days when I was twenty-one.

Let us begone—the place is sad and strange;
　　How far, far off those happy times appear;
All that I have to live I'd gladly change
　　For one such month as I have wasted here—
To draw long dreams of beauty, love, and power
　　From founts of hope that never will return,
And drink all life's quintessence in an hour—
　　Give me the days when I was twenty-one!

ON A GIRDLE.

BY EDMUND WALLER.

That which her slender waist confined
Shall now my joyful temples bind:
No monarch but would give his crown
His arms might do what this hath done.

It was my heaven's extremest sphere,
The pale which held that lovely deer:
My joy, my grief, my hope, my love
Did all within this circle move.

A narrow compass! and yet there
Dwelt all that's good, and all that's fair:
Give me but what this ribband bound,
Take all the rest the sun goes round.

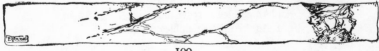

SOLILOQUY FROM MACBETH.

BY WILLIAM SHAKSPEARE.

Tomorrow, and tomorrow, and tomorrow,
Creeps in this petty pace from day to day
To the last syllable of recorded time,
And all our yesterdays have lighted fools
The way to dusty death.   Out, out, brief candle!
Life's but a walking shadow, a poor player
That struts and frets his hour upon the stage
And then is heard no more; it is a tale
Told by an idiot, full of sound and fury,
Signifying nothing.

THE DAY IS DONE.

BY HENRY WADSWORTH LONGFELLOW.

The day is done, and the darkness
    Falls from the wings of Night,
As a feather is wafted downward
    From an eagle in his flight.

I see the lights of the village
    Gleam through the rain and the mist,
And a feeling of sadness comes o'er me
    That my soul cannot resist;

A feeling of sadness and longing
    That is not akin to pain,
And resembles sorrow only
    As the mist resembles the rain.

Come, read to me some poem,
　　Some simple and heartfelt lay,
That shall soothe this restless feeling,
　　And banish the thoughts of day.

Not from the grand old masters,
　　Not from the bards sublime,
Whose distant footsteps echo
　　Through the corridors of Time.

For, like strains of martial music,
　　Their mighty thoughts suggest
Life's endless toil and endeavor;
　　And to-night I long for rest.

Read from some humbler poet,
　　Whose songs gushed from his heart
As showers from the clouds of summer
　　Or tears from the eyelids start;

Who through long days of labor
　　And nights devoid of ease,
Still heard in his soul the music
　　Of wonderful melodies.

Such songs have power to quiet
　　The restless pulse of care,
And come like the benediction
　　That follows after prayer.

Then read from the treasured volume
　　The poem of thy choice,
And lend to the rhyme of the poet
　　The beauty of thy voice.

And the night shall be filled with music,
　　And the cares that infest the day
Shall fold their tents, like the Arabs,
　　And as silently steal away.

LITTLE BREECHES.

BY JOHN HAY.

I don't go much on religion,
  I never ain't had no show;
But I've got a middlin' tight grip, sir,
  On the handful o' things I know.
I don't pan out on the prophets,
  And free-will, and that sort of thing—
But I b'lieve in God and the angels
  Ever sence one night last spring.

I come into town with some turnips,
  And my little Gabe come along—
No four-year-old in the county
  Could beat him for pretty and strong,
Peart, and chippy, and sassy,
  Always ready to swear and fight—
And I'd larnt him to chaw terbacker
  Jest to keep his milk-teeth white.

The snow come down like a blanket
  As I passed by Taggart's store;
I went in for a jug of molasses
  And left the team at the door.
They scared at something and started—
  I heard one little squall
And hell-to-split over the prairie
  Went team, Little Breeches and all.

Hell-to-split over the prairie!
  I was almost froze with skeer;

But we rousted up some torches
   And sarched for 'em far and near.
At last we struck hosses and wagon
   Snowed under a soft, white mound,
Upsot, dead beat—but of little Gabe
   No hide nor hair was found.

And here all hope soured on me,
   Of my fellow-critter's aid—
I jest flopped down on my marrow-bones,
   Crotch deep in the snow and prayed.

*   *   *   *   *   *   *   *   *

By this, the torches was played out,
   And me and Isrul Parr
Went off for some wood to a sheepfold
   That he said was somewhar thar.

We found it at last, and a little shed
   Where they shut up the lambs at night.
We looked in and seen them huddled thar,
   So warm, and sleepy, and white,
And thar sot Little Breeches and chirped,
   As peart as ever you see,
"I want a chaw of terbacker,
   And that's what the matter of me."

How did he git thar? Angels.
   He could never have walked in that storm;
They jest stooped down and toted him
   To whar it was safe and warm.
And I think that saving a little child,
   And fotching him to his own,
Is a durned sight better business
   Than loafing around the Throne.

FLYNN OF VIRGINIA.

BY BRET HARTE.

Didn't know Flynn—
Flynn of Virginia—
 Long as he's been 'yar?
 Look'ee here, stranger
Whar hev you been?

Here in this tunnel
He was my pardner,
That same Tom Flynn—
 Working together,
 In wind and weather,
Day out and in.

Didn't know Flynn!
 Well, that is queer.
Why, it's a sin,
To think of Tom Flynn—
 Tom, with his cheer;
 Tom, without fear—
Stranger, look 'yar!

Thar in the drift,
 Back to the wall,
He held the timbers
 Ready to fall;
Then in the darkness
 I heard him call:
"Run for your life, Jake!
Run for your wife's sake!

Don't wait for me."
And that was all
    Heard in the din,
    Heard of Tom Flynn—
Flynn of Virginia.

That lets me out
    Here in the damp—
Out of the sun—
    That 'ar derned lamp
Makes my eyes run.
Well, there—I'm done.

But, sir, when you'll
Hear the next fool
Asking of Flynn—
Flynn of Virginia—
    Just you chip in,
    Say you knew Flynn;
Say that you've been 'yar.

WARBLE FOR LILAC-TIME.

BY WALT WHITMAN.

Warble me now for joy of lilac-time,
Sort me, O tongue and lips for nature's sake, souvenirs of
    earliest summer,
Gather the welcome signs (as children with pebbles of string-
    ing shells),
Put in April and May, the hylas croaking in the ponds, the
    elastic air,
Bees, butterflies, the sparrow with its simple notes,
Bluebird and darting swallow, nor forget the high-hole flash-
    ing his golden wings,
The tranquil sunny haze, the clinging smoke, the vapor,
Shimmer of waters with fish in them, the cerulean above.
All that is jocund and sparkling, the brooks running,
The maple woods, the crisp February days and the sugar
    making,
The robin where he hops, bright-eyed, brown-breasted,
With musical clear call at sunrise and again at sunset.
Or flitting among the trees of the apple orchard, building the
    nest of his mate,
The melted snow of March, the willow sending forth its yel-
    low-green sprouts,
For springtime is here! The summer is here, and what is this
    in it and from it?
Thou, soul, unloosen'd—the restlessness after I know not what;
Come, let us lag here no longer, let us be up and away!
O, if one could fly like a bird!
O, to escape, to sail forth as in a ship!

To glide with thee, O soul, o'er all, in all, as a ship o'er the
    waters;
Gathering these hints, the preludes, the blue sky, the grass, the
    morning drops of dew,
The lilac-scent, the bushes with dark green heart-shaped leaves,
Wood violets, the little delicate pale blossoms called innocent
Samples and sorts not for themselves alone, but for their
    atmosphere
To grace the bush I love—to sing with the birds,
A warble for joy of lilac-time.

PORTIA'S SPEECH ON MERCY.

BY WILLIAM SHAKSPEARE.

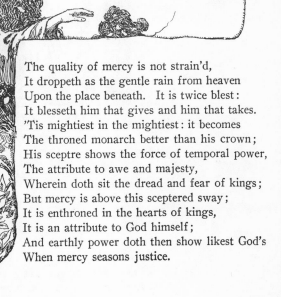

The quality of mercy is not strain'd,
It droppeth as the gentle rain from heaven
Upon the place beneath.   It is twice blest:
It blesseth him that gives and him that takes.
'Tis mightiest in the mightiest: it becomes
The throned monarch better than his crown;
His sceptre shows the force of temporal power,
The attribute to awe and majesty,
Wherein doth sit the dread and fear of kings;
But mercy is above this sceptered sway;
It is enthroned in the hearts of kings,
It is an attribute to God himself;
And earthly power doth then show likest God's
When mercy seasons justice.

207

THE PARADOX OF TIME.

BY AUSTIN DOBSON.

Time goes, you say? Ah, no!
Alas! Time stays, we go;
　Or else, were this not so,
What need to chain the hours,
For youth were always ours?
　Time goes, you say?—ah, no!

Ours is the eyes' deceit
Of men whose flying feet
　Lead through some landscape low;

We pass, and think we see
The earth's fixed surface flee;
   Alas! Time stays—we go!

Once, in the days of old,
Your locks were curling gold,
   And mine had shamed the crow;
Now, in the self-same stage,
We've reached the silver age;
   Time goes, you say?—ah, no!

Once, when my voice was strong,
I filled the woods with song
   To praise your "rose" and "snow";
My bird that sung is dead;
Where are your roses fled?
   Alas! Time stays—we go!

See in what traversed ways,
What backward fate delays
   The hopes we used to know;
Where are our old desires—
Ah! where those vanished fires?
   Time goes, you say?—ah, no!

How far, how far, O sweet,
The past behind our feet
   Lies in the even-glow!
Now, on the forward way,
Let us fold hands and pray;
   Alas! Time stays—we go!

NOCTURNE.

BY THOMAS BAILEY ALDRICH.

Up to her chamber window,
   A slight wire trellis goes,
And up this Romeo ladder
   Clambers a bold white rose.
I lounge in the ilex shadows,
   I see the lady lean,
Unclasping her silken girdle,
   The curtain's folds between.

She smiles on her white-rose lover,
   She reaches out her hand
And helps him in at the window—
   I see it where I stand!
To her scarlet lip she holds him,
   And kisses him many a time—
Ah me! It was he that won her
   Because he dared to climb.

THE SOCIETY UPON THE STANISLAUS.

BY BRET HARTE.

I reside at Table Mountain and my name is Truthful James;
I am not up to small deceit or any sinful games;
And I'll tell in simple language what I know about the row
That broke up our society upon the Stanislow.

But first I would remark that it is not a proper plan
For any scientific gent to whale his fellow man,
And if a member don't agree with his peculiar whim
To lay for that same member for to "put a head" on him.

Now nothing could be finer or more beautiful to see
Than the first six months' proceedings of that same society,
Till Brown of Calaveras brought a lot of fossil bones
That he found within a tunnel near the tenement of Jones.

Then Brown he read a paper, and he reconstructed there,
From those same bones an animal that was extremely rare;
And Jones then asked the chair for a suspension of the rules
Till he could prove that those same bones was one of his lost
     mules.

Then Brown he smiled a bitter smile, and said he was at fault,
It seems he had been trespassing on Jones' family vault;
He was a most sarcastic man, this quiet Mr. Brown,
And on several occasions he had cleaned out the town.

Now I hold it is not decent for a scientific gent
To say another is an ass—at least, to all intent;
Nor should the individual who happens to be meant
Reply by heaving rocks at him to any great extent.

Then Abner Dean of Angel's raised a point of order when—
A chunk of old red sandstone took him in the abdomen,
And he smiled a kind of sickly smile and curled up on the floor,
And the subsequent proceedings interested him no more.

For, in less time than I write it, every member did engage
In a warfare with the remnants of a paleozoic age;
And the way they heaved those fossils in their anger was a sin,
Till the skull of an old mammoth caved the head of Thompson
     in.

——— And this is all I have to say of these
     improper games,
For I live at Table Mountain and
     my name is Truthful James;
And I've told in simple language
     what I know about the row
That broke up our society upon the
     Stanislow.

NATHAN HALE.

BY FRANCIS MILES FINCH.

These verses were written by the author of "The Blue and the Gray."
Nathan Hale, great-uncle of Edward Everett Hale, was born at Coventry, Conn., June 6, 1755. He was sent to New York by Washington to get information about the British, and was arrested while on that mission. He was hanged as a spy by order of Sir William Howe, Sept. 22, 1776. By his executioner he was denied the use of a Bible, and his family letters were burned.

To drum beat and heart beat,
   A soldier marches by;
There is color in his cheek,
   There is courage in his eye,
Yet to drum beat and heart beat
   In a moment he must die.

By the starlight and moonlight,
   He seeks the Briton's camp;
He hears the rustling flag
   And the armed sentry's tramp;
And the starlight and the moonlight
   His silent wanderings lamp.

With slow tread and still tread,
   He scans the tented line;
And he counts the battery guns,
   By the gaunt and shadowy pine;
And his slow tread and still tread
   Gives no warning sign.

The dark wave, the plumed wave,
   It meets his eager glance;
And it sparkles 'neath the stars,
   Like the glimmer of a lance—
A dark wave, a plumed wave,
   On an emerald expanse.

A sharp clang, a still clang,
   And terror in the sound!
For the sentry, falcon eyed,
   In the camp a spy hath found;
With a sharp clang, a steel clang,
   The patriot is bound.

With a calm brow and a steady brow,
   He listens to his doom;
In his look there is no fear,
   Nor a shadowy trace of gloom;
But with calm brow and steady brow,
   He robes him for the tomb.

In the long night, the still night,
   He kneels upon the sod;
And the brutal guards withhold
   E'en the solemn word of God!
In the long night, the still night,
   He walks where Christ hath trod.

'Neath the blue morn, the sunny morn,
   He dies upon the tree;
And he mourns that he can lose
   But one life for liberty;
And in the blue morn, the sunny morn,
   His spent wings are free.

But his last words, his message words,
   They burn, lest friendly eye
Should read how proud and calm
   A patriot could die.
With his last words, his dying words,
   A soldier's battle cry.

From fame leaf and angel leaf,
   From monument and urn,
The sad earth, the glad of heaven,
   His tragic fate shall learn;
And on fame leaf and angel leaf
   The name of HALE shall burn!

THE SONG OF CALLICLES.

BY MATTHEW ARNOLD.

Through the black, rushing smoke-bursts
    Thick breaks the red flame.
All Etna heaves fiercely
    Her forest-clothed flame.

Not here, O, Apollo,
    Are haunts meet for thee,
But where Helicon breaks down
    In cliff to the sea.

Where the moon-silver'd inlets
    Send far their light voice
Up the still vale of Thisbe,
    O, speed, and rejoice!

On the sward at the cliff-top
    Lie strewn the white flocks;
On the cliff-side the pigeons
    Roost deep in the rocks.

In the moonlight the shepherds,
    Soft-lull'd by the rills,
Lie wrapped in their blankets,
    Asleep on the hills.

What forms are those coming,
    So white through the gloom?
What garments out-glistening
    The gold-flower'd broom?

What sweet-breathing Presence
    Out-perfumes the thyme?
What voices enrapture
    The night's balmy prime?

'Tis Apollo comes leading
    His choir, the Nine—
The Leader is fairest,
    But all are divine.

They are lost in the hollow,
    They stream up again.
What seeks on this mountain
    The glorified train?

They bathe in this mountain,
    In the spring by their road.
Then on to Olympus,
    Their endless abode.

Whose praise do they mention?
    Of what is it told,
What will be forever,
    What was from of old.

First hymn they the Father
    Of all things; and then,
The rest of Immortals,
    The action of men.

The Day in his hotness,
    The strife with the palm;
The Night in her silence,
    The Stars in their calm.

SONG FROM "MARMION."

BY SIR WALTER SCOTT.

Where shall the lover rest,
  Whom the fates sever
From his true maiden's breast,
  Parted forever?
Where through groves deep and high,
  Sounds the far billow,
Where early violets die,
  Under the willow.

There, through the summer day,
  Cool streams are laving;
There, while the tempests sway,
  Scarce are boughs waving.
There thy rest shalt thou take,
  Parted forever,
Never again to wake,
  Never, O, never!

Where shall the traitor rest,
  He, the deceiver,
Who could win maiden's breast,
  Ruin and leave her?
In the lost battle,
  Borne down by the flying,
Where mingles war's rattle
  With groans of the dying.

Her wing shall the eagle flap,
  O'er the false hearted.

His warm blood the wolf shall lap,
  E'er life be parted.
Shame and dishonor sit
  By his grave ever;
Blessing shall hallow it—
  Never, O, never!

THE GRASS.
BY EMILY DICKINSON.

The grass so little has to do—
A sphere of simple green,
With only butterflies to brood,
And bees to entertain,

And stir all day to pretty tunes
The breezes fetch along,
And hold the sunshine in its lap
And bow to everything;

And thread the dews all night, like pearls,
And make itself so fine—
A duchess were too common
For such a noticing.

And even when it dies, to pass
In odors so divine,
As lowly spices gone to sleep,
Or amulets of pine.

And then to dwell in sovereign barns,
And dream the days away—
The grass so little has to do,
I wish I were the hay!

217

THE WIDOW MALONE.

BY CHARLES LEVER.

Charles James Lever was born at Dublin in 1806. He was a graduate of Trinity College, Dublin, and afterwards became a physician, as well as a journalist, and the editor of the Dublin University Magazine. He was consul at Spezzia in 1858, and later at Trieste, where he died in 1872. His poems, when he did'not try to be serious, are full of humor and rhythm. He wrote, among other novels, "Harry Lorrequer," "Charles O'Malley," and "Tom Burke of Ours."

Did you hear of the Widow Malone,
      Ohone!
Who lived in the town of Athlone,
      Alone?
Oh! she melted the hearts
Of the swains in them parts—
So lovely the Widow Malone,
      Ohone!
So lovely the Widow Malone.

Of lovers she had a full score
      Or more;
And fortunes they all had galore,
      In store;
From the minister down
To the clerk of the crown,
All were courting the Widow Malone,
      Ohone!
All were courting the Widow Malone.

But so modest was Mistress Malone,
      'Twas known
That no one could see her alone,
      Ohone!

Let them ogle and sigh,
They could ne'er catch her eye—
So bashful the Widow Malone,
        Ohone!
So bashful the Widow Malone.

Till one Misther O'Brien from Clare—
        How quare!
It's little for blushing they care
        Down there—
Put his arm round her waist,
Gave ten kisses at laste—
"Oh," says he, "you're my Molly Malone—
        My own!"
"Oh," says he, "you're my Molly Malone!"

And the widow they all thought so shy,
        My eye!
Ne'er thought of a simper or sigh—
        For why?
But, "Lucius," says she,
"Since you've now made so free,
You may marry your Mary Malone,
        Ohone!
You may marry your Mary Malone."

There's a moral contained in my song,
        Not wrong,
And, one comfort, it's not very long,
        But strong;
If for widows you die
Learn to kiss, not to sigh,
For they're all like sweet Mistress Malone!
        Ohone!
Oh! they're all like sweet Mistress Malone!

MY WIFE AND CHILD.
BY GENERAL HENRY R. JACKSON.

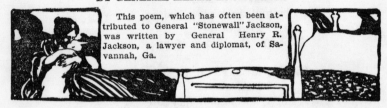

This poem, which has often been attributed to General "Stonewall" Jackson, was written by General Henry R. Jackson, a lawyer and diplomat, of Savannah, Ga.

The tattoo beats—the lights are gone,
 The camp around in slumber lies;
The night with solemn pace moves on,
 The shadows thicken o'er the skies;
But sleep my weary eyes hath flown,
 And sad, uneasy thoughts arise.

I think of thee, Oh, dearest one,
 Whose love my early life hath blest—
Of thee and him—our baby son—
 Who slumbers on thy gentle breast.
God of the tender, frail and lone,
 Oh, guard the tender sleeper's rest.

And hover gently, hover near,
 To her, whose watchful eye is wet—
To mother, wife—the doubly dear,
In whose young heart have freshly met
Two streams of love so deep and clear
 And clear her drooping spirits yet.

Whatever fate those forms may show,
 Loved with a passion almost wild—
By day—by night—in joy or woe—
 By fears oppressed, or hopes beguiled,
From every danger, every foe,
 O God! protect my wife and child!

Now, while she kneels before Thy throne,
 Oh, teach her, ruler of the skies,
That, while by thy behest alone,

Earth's mightiest powers fall or rise,
No tear is wept to Thee unknown,
  No hair is lost, no sparrow dies!

That Thou can'st stay the ruthless hands
  Of dark disease, and soothe its pain;
That only by Thy stern command
  The battle's lost, the soldier's slain—
That from the distant sea or land
  Thou bring'st the wanderer home again.

And when upon her pillow lone
  Her tear-wet cheek is sadly prest,
May happier visions beam upon
  The brightening current of her breast,
No frowning look nor angry tone
  Disturb the Sabbath of her rest.

JONATHAN TO JOHN.

BY JAMES RUSSELL LOWELL.

Lowell was born at Cambridge, Mass., in 1819. He went to Harvard college and was Longfellow's successor as professor of modern languages at the same college. From 1857-'62 he was editor of the Atlantic Monthly; in 1863-'72 he was editor of the North American Review. He held the office of United States minister, first to Spain—1877-'80—and later to Great Britain—1880-'85. Lowell died at Cambridge in 1891. Among his poems are the "Biglow Papers," the "Vision of Sir Launfal," "A Tale for Critics." Some of his prose works are "Among My Books," "My Study Windows," and "Political Essays."

It don't seem hardly right, John,
    When both my hands was full,
To stump me to a fight, John—
    Your cousin, tu, John Bull!
Ole Uncle S., sez he, "I guess
    We know it now," sez he;
"The lion's paw is all the law,
    According to J. B.,
    Thet's fit for you an' 'me!"

You wonder why we're hot, John?
    Your mark wuz on the guns—
The neutral guns, thet shot, John,
    Our brothers an' our sons.
Ole Uncle S., sez he, "I guess
    There's human blood," sez he,
"By fits an' starts, in Yankee hearts,
    Though 't may surprise J. B.
    More 'n it would you an' me."

When your rights was our wrongs, John,
    You didn't stop for fuss—
Britanny's trident prongs, John,
    Was good 'nough law for us.
Ole Uncle S., sez he, "I guess,
    Though physic's good," sez he,
"It doesn't foller thet he can swaller
    Prescriptions signed 'J. B.',
    Put up by you an' me!"

We own the ocean, tu, John;
　　You mus'n't take it hard,
Ef we can't think with you, John,
　　It's jest your own back yard.
Ole Uncle S., sez he, "I guess,
　　Ef thet's his claim," sez he,
'The fencin' stuff'll cost enough
　　To bust up friend J. B.,
　　Ez wal ez you an' me!"

We know we've got a cause, John,
　　Thet's honest, just, an' true;
We thought 'twould win applause, John,
　　Ef nowheres else, from you.
Ole Uncle S., sez he, "I guess
　　His love of right," sez he,
"Hangs by a rotten fibre o' cotton;
　　There's natur' in J. B.,
　　Ez wal ez you an' me!"

God means to make this land, John,
　　Clear thru, from sea to sea,
Believe an' understand, John,
　　The wuth o' being free.
Ole Uncle S., sez he, "I guess
　　God's price is high," sez he;
"But nothin' else than wut he sells
　　Wears long, an' thet J. B.
　　May larn, like you an' me."

SOLILOQUY FROM "HAMLET."

BY WILLIAM SHAKSPEARE.

To be, or not to be; that is the question;
Whether 'tis nobler in the mind to suffer
The slings and arrows of outrageous fortune,
Or to take arms against a sea of troubles,
And by opposing end them? To die: to sleep:
No more; and by a sleep to say we end
The heart-ache and the thousand natural shocks
That flesh is heir to; 'tis a consummation
Devoutly to be wished. To die; to sleep;
To sleep: perchance to dream: aye, there's the rub;
For in that sleep of death what dreams may come,
When we have shuffled off this mortal coil,
Must give us pause: there's the respect
That makes calamity of so long life;
For who would bear the whips and scorns of time,
The oppressor's wrong, the proud man's contumely,
The pangs of despis'd love, the law's delay,
The insolence of office, and the spurns
That patient merit of the unworthy takes,
When he himself might his quietus make
With a bare bodkin? Who would fardels bear,
To grunt and sweat under a weary life,
But that the dread of something after death—
The undiscover'd country from whose bourn
No traveler returns—puzzles the will
And makes us rather bear those ills we have
Than fly to others that we know not of?
Thus conscience does make cowards of us all,
And thus the native hue of resolution
Is sicklied o'er with the pale cast of thought,
And enterprises of great pith and moment
With this regard their currents turns awry
And lose the name of action.

TO A WATER FOWL.

BY WILLIAM CULLEN BRYANT.

Whither, 'midst falling dew,
   While glow the heavens with the last steps of day,
Far, through their rosy depths, dost thou pursue
   Thy solitary way?

Vainly the fowler's eye
   Might mark thy distant flight to do thee wrong,
As, darkly painted on the crimson sky,
   Thy figure floats along.

     *   *   *   *   *   *   *

There is a power whose care
   Teaches thy way along that pathless coast—
The desert and illimitable air—
   Lone wandering, but not lost.

All day thy wings have fanned,
   At that far height, the cold, thin atmosphere.
Yet stoop not, weary, to the welcome land,
   Though the dark night is near.

     *   *   *   *   *   *   *

Thou'rt gone; the abyss of heaven
   Hath swallowed up thy form; yet on my heart
Deeply hath sunk the lesson thou hast given,
   And shall not soon depart.

He who, from zone to zone,
   Guides through the boundless sky thy certain flight,
In the long way that I must tread alone
   Will lead my steps aright.

ANTONY AND CLEOPATRA.

BY GENL. WILLIAM H. LYTLE.

William Haines Lytle was born at Cincinnati, O., in 1826, and died a hero's death at Chickamauga in 1863. He enlisted in the Mexican war in 1846, and served with distinction. Afterwards he attained prominence as a lawyer and politician. When the civil war broke out he was appointed major general of volunteers. At Carnifex ferry he was desperately wounded, but recovered and took charge of a brigade. He was again wounded at Perryville and captured. Being exchanged, he was promoted to brigadier general and fought in many engagements till Sept. 29, 1863. His poems were never collected in book form. This one was written in 1857.

I am dying, Egypt, dying!
  Ebbs the crimson life-tide fast,
And the dark Plutonian shadows
  Gather on the evening blast.
Let thine arms, O queen, enfold me;
  Hush thy sobs and bow thine ear.
Listen to the great heart secrets
  Thou, and thou alone, must hear.

Though my scarred and veteran legions
  Bear their eagles high no more,
And my wrecked and scattered galleys
  Strew dark Actium's fatal shore;
Though no glittering guards surround me,
  Prompt to do their master's will,
I must perish like a Roman—
  Die the great Triumvir still!

Let no Cæsar's servile minions
  Mock the lion thus laid low;
'Twas no foeman's arm that felled him;
  'Twas his own that struck the blow—
His who, pillowed on thy bosom,
  Turned aside from glory's ray—
His who, drunk with thy caresses,
  Madly threw a world away.

Should the base plebeian rabble
  Dare assail my name at Rome,
Where my noble spouse, Octavia,
  Weeps within her widowed home,
Seek her; say the gods bear witness—
  Altars, augurs, circling wings—
That her blood with mine commingled,
  Yet shall mount the throne of kings.

As for thee, star-eyed Egyptian!
  Glorious sorceress of the Nile!
Light the path to Stygian horrors
  With the splendors of thy smile.
Give to Cæsar crowns and arches,
  Let his brow the laurel twine;
I can scorn the senate's triumphs,
  Triumphing in love like thine.

I am dying, Egypt, dying;
  Hark! the insulting foeman's cry.
They are coming—quick, my falchion!
  Let me front them ere I die.
Ah! no more amid the battle
  Shall my heart exulting swell;
Isis and Osiris guard thee!
  Cleopatra—Rome—farewell!

O, WHY SHOULD THE SPIRIT OF MORTAL BE PROUD?

BY WILLIAM KNOX.

The following poem was a particular favorite with Abraham Lincoln. It was first shown to him when a young man by a friend, and afterwards he cut it from a newspaper and learned it by heart. He said to a friend: "I would give a great deal to know who wrote it, but have never been able to ascertain." He did afterwards learn the name of the author.

William Knox was a Scottish poet who was born in 1789 at Firth and died in 1825 at Edinburgh. His "Lonely Hearth and Other Poems" was published in 1818, and "The Songs of Israel," from which "O, Why Should the Spirit of Mortal be Proud" is taken, in 1824. Sir Walter Scott was an admirer of Knox's poems, and befriended the author when his habits brought him into need.

O, why should the spirit of mortal be proud?
Like a swift-fleeting meteor, a fast-flying cloud,
A flash of the lightning, a break of the wave,
Man passeth from life to his rest in the grave.

The leaves of the oak and the willow shall fade,
Be scattered around, and together be laid;
As the young and the old, the low and the high,
Shall crumble to dust and together shall lie.

The infant a mother attended and loved,
The mother that infant's affection who proved,
The father that mother and infant who blest—
Each, all, are away to that dwelling of rest.

The maid on whose brow, on whose cheek, in whose eye,
Shone beauty and pleasure—her triumphs are by;
And alike from the minds of the living erased
Are the memories of mortals who loved her and praised.

The head of the King, that the scepter hath borne;
The brow of the priest, that the miter hath worn;
The eye of the sage, and the heart of the brave—
Are hidden and lost in the depths of the grave.

The peasant whose lot was to sow and to reap;
The herdsman, who climbed with his goats up the steep;
The beggar, who wandered in search of his bread—
Have faded away like the grass that we tread.

So the multitude goes, like the flower or the weed,
That withers away to let others succeed;
So the multitude comes, even those we behold,
To repeat every tale that has often been told.

For we are the same our fathers have been;
We see the same sights our fathers have seen;
We drink the same stream, we see the same sun,
And run the same course our fathers have run.

The thoughts we are thinking our fathers did think;
From the death we are shrinking our fathers did shrink;
To the life we are clinging our fathers did cling,
But it speeds from us all like the bird on the wing.

They loved—but the story we cannot unfold;
They scorned—but the heart of the haughty is cold;
They grieved—but no wail from their slumbers will come;
They joyed—but the tongue of their gladness is dumb.

They died—ah! they died—we, things that are now,
That walk on the turf that lies over their brow,
And make in their dwelling a transient abode,
Meet the things that they met on their pilgrimage road.

Yea, hope and despondency, pleasure and pain,
Are mingled together in sunshine and rain,
And the smile and the tear, and the song and the dirge,
Still follow each other like surge upon surge.

'Tis the wink of an eye; 'tis the draught of a breath,
From the blossom of health to the paleness of death,
From the gilded saloon to the bier and the shroud;
O, why should the spirit of mortal be proud?

THE THREE FISHERS.

BY CHARLES KINGSLEY.

Charles Kingsley was born in Devonshire in 1819; he died in 1875.
His poetical works consist of "The Saint's Tragedy" and "Andromeda
and Other Poems."

Three fishers went sailing out into the West,
  Out into the West as the sun went down;
Each thought on the woman who loved him the best;
  And the children stood watching them out of the town;
    For men must work and women must weep,
    And there's little to earn, and many to keep,
      Though the harbor bar be moaning.

Three wives sat up in the lighthouse tower,
  And they trimmed the lamps as the sun went down;
They looked at the squall and they looked at the shower,
  And the rack it came rolling up ragged and brown!
    But men must work and women must weep,
    Though storms be sudden and waters deep,
      And the harbor bar be moaning.

Three corpses lay out on the shining sands
  In the morning gleam as the tide went down,
And the women are weeping and wringing their hands
  For those who will never come back to the town;
    For men must work and women must weep,
    And the sooner it's over, the sooner to sleep—
      And good-by to the bar and its moaning.

230

PSALM XLVIII.

Great is the Lord, and greatly to be praised
In the city of our God, in the mountain of his holiness,
Beautiful for situation, the joy of the whole earth,
Is Mount Zion, on the sides of the north, the city of the great
      King.
God is known in her palaces for a refuge,
For, lo, the kings were assembled,
They passed by together.
They saw it and so they marveled;
They were troubled, and hasted away.
Fear took hold upon them there,
And pain, as of a woman in travail.
Thou breakest the ships of Tarshish with an east wind,
As we have heard, so have we seen
In the city of the Lord of hosts, in the city of our God;
God will establish it forever.
We have thought of thy lovingkindness, O God,
In the midst of thy temple.
According to thy name, O God,
So is thy praise unto the ends of the earth;
Thy right hand is full of righteousness.
Let Mount Zion rejoice,
Let the daughters of Judah be glad, because of thy judgments.
Walk about Zion, and go round about her;
Tell the towers thereof.
Mark ye well her bulwarks, consider her palaces;
That ye may tell it to the generation following.
For this God is our God for ever and ever;
He will be our guide even unto death.

THE ISLES OF GREECE.

BY LORD BYRON.

The isles of Greece, the isles of Greece!
  Where burning Sappho loved and sung,
Where grew the arts of war and peace—
  Where Delos rose and Phœbus sprung!
Eternal summer gilds them yet,
But all except their sun, is set.

The mountains look on Marathon—
  And Marathon looks on the sea;
And, musing there an hour alone,
I dream'd that Greece might still be free;
For standing on the Persians' grave
I could not deem myself a slave.

A King sate on the rocky brow
  Which looks o'er sea-born Salamis;
And ships, by thousands, lay below,
  And men in nations—all were his!
He counted them at break of day—
And when the sun set where were they?

And where are they? and where art thou,
  My country? On thy voiceless shore
The heroic lay is tuneless now—
  The heroic bosom beats no more!
And must thy lyre, so long divine,
Degenerate into hands like mine?

Must we but weep o'er days more blest?
  Must we but blush? Our father's bled.
Earth! render back from out thy breast
  A remnant of our Spartan dead!
Of the three hundred grant but three,
To make a new Thermopylæ!

In vain—in vain: strike other chords;
　　Fill high the cup with Samian wine!
Leave battles to the Turkish hordes,
　　And shed the blood of Scio's vine!
Hark! rising to the ignoble call—
How answers each bold Bacchanal!

You have the Pyrrhic dance as yet,
　　Where is the Pyrrhic phalanx gone?
Of two such lessons, why forget
　　The nobler and the manlier one?
You have the letters Cadmus gave—
Think ye he meant them for a slave?

Fill high the bowl with Samian wine!
　　Our virgins dance beneath the shade—
I see their glorious black eyes shine!
　　But gazing on each glowing maid,
My own the burning tear-drop laves,
To think such breasts must suckle slaves.

Place me on Sunium's marbled steep
　　Where nothing, save the waves and I,
　　　　May hear our mutual murmurs
　　　　　　sweep;
　　　　　There, swan-like, let me sing
　　　　　　and die:
　　　　A land of slaves shall ne'er be
　　　　　　mine—
　　　　Dash down yon cup of Samian
　　　　　　wine!

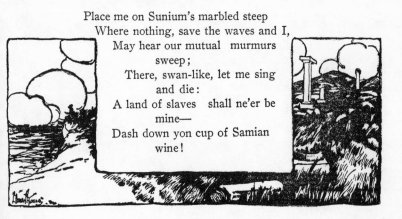

INDEX